MAKE & DO

QUICK & EASY

Introduction

Hooked on Crochet is perfect for beginners, as well as for crocheters hoping to improve their technique. It also serves as an excellent reference for anyone with more advanced skills.

This easy-to-follow guide takes you through basic techniques and stitches, covering the relevant abbreviations and symbols on the way. Beautiful projects to make, woven in among the techniques, will inspire you while a final section covers useful finishing techniques such as stitching seams, sewing on buttons, and making fringes.

If you're new to crochet, start by familiarizing yourself with the tools and materials. Then move on to the Techniques and Projects section, where you first learn how to make a slip knot and create a foundation chain. You will then be taken through the most common crochet stitches as well as the ins and outs of reading crochet patterns.

As well as how-to help, there are more than 20 projects to practise your skills. Or for more advanced crocheters, you can turn straight to the patterns and make lovely projects for yourself or to give as gifts. Projects range from cosy cushions and blankets to desirable scarves and toys.

All you need are yarn and hooks and you're ready to be creative!

GREAT IDEAS

Page **28**

Page **50**

Content

LONDON, NEW YORK, MELBOURNE,
MUNICH, AND DELHI

Designed by Clare Shedden, Saskia Janssen
Edited by Emma Callery, Elizabeth Yeates
Senior Jacket Creative Nicola Powling
Special Sales Creative Project Manager Alison Donovan
Pre Production Producer Rebecca Fallowfield
Senior Producer Katherine Whyte

PERFECT GIFTS

Page 126

First published in Great Britain in 2014
by Dorling Kindersley Limited
80 Strand, London WC2R 0RL

A Penguin Random House Company

Previously published as Cute Crochet (2013)

Copyright © 2013, 2014 Dorling Kindersley Limited

A CIP catalogue record for this book
is available from the British Library.

ISBN 978-0-2411-8604-6

Printed and bound in Italy
by L.E.G.O. S.p.A.

**Discover more at
www.dk.com/crafts**

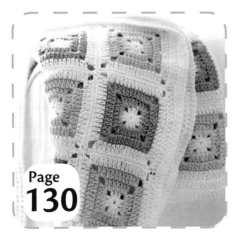

Page 130

Tools and materials

Yarns

A yarn is the long, stranded, spun fibre that we crochet with. There are many types of yarns, allowing crocheters to enjoy a variety of sensory experiences as they express themselves through the medium. Yarns can be made of many different fibres (see pp.10–12) and have a range of textures (see p.13). Their possibilities are exciting: you can, in theory, crochet with anything – from a skein of supple sock yarn to the plastic bag that you brought it home in. Choose from a colour palette that ranges from subtle, muted tones to eye-popping brights.

Cotton yarns

Cotton crochet threads
Traditionally, crochet was worked in cotton threads that were suitable for lace. Today, cotton threads are still used for lace edgings (see pp.86–89) and filet crochet.

Fine-weight cotton yarns
This thicker yarn is a good weight for garments and accessories and will show the texture of stitch patterns clearly.

Mercerized cotton
Cotton fibre can be mercerized, a treatment during which it undergoes mechanical and chemical processing to compress it and transform it into an ultra-strong yarn with a reflective sheen. It is a fine choice of fibre for a project that needs to be strong and hold its shape, such as a clutch bag (see pp.64–65), a long summer cardigan, or a throw.

Matt cotton
Cotton is the fluffy mass that grows around the seeds of the cotton plant. It is spun into a breathable, summery fibre. Most cotton yarns are easy to wash, and when cared for correctly, can be incredibly robust and last for decades. It is therefore a good fibre for homewares, crocheted pouches, and shoulder bags. Pure, untreated cotton is ideal for hand-dyeing.

Wool

Wool

The hair, or fleece, of a variety of breeds of sheep, such as the Shetland Moorit or Bluefaced Leicester, is made into pure wool yarns, or blended with other fibres. It is very warm and hard-wearing, and great for winter wear such as jackets, cardigans, hats, and gloves. Some wool is rough, but softens with wear and washing. Wool sold as "organic" contains a high proportion of lanolin, making a strong, waterproof yarn.

Merino wool

This is wool from the merino sheep, which is said to provide one of the softest wools of any sheep breed. The bouncy, smooth-surfaced fibre is just as warm as a more wiry, coarse wool. Merino is a fantastic choice for wearing against the skin, and is often treated to make it suitable for machine-washing. Good for soft scarves, arm warmers, and children's garments.

Other natural fibres

Hemp

The hemp plant is particularly versatile, and the use of its fibres for knitting yarn is one of its less common applications. Hemp has an earthy roughness that will soften with age and wear. It is usually produced in an environmentally friendly way, and the strong fibre is good for crocheting openwork shopping bags and homewares such as placemats and coasters.

Ramie

A plant from the nettle family yields the fibre called ramie. The bark of the plant is dried out into workable fibres, which are then spun into yarns. Like other plant fibres, this yarn does not insulate; it is desirable for its strength and airy quality. It is frequently blended with other fibres to produce a yarn that is breathable and wears well.

Yarns, like fabrics, are made from fibres. A fibre may be the hair from an animal, man-made (synthetics), or derived from a plant. The fibres are processed and spun to make a yarn. A yarn may be made from a single type of fibre, such as wool, or mixed with other fibres to enhance its attributes (for example, to affect its durability or softness). Different blends are also created for aesthetic reasons, such as mixing soft, luxurious cashmere with a rougher wool. As a result, all yarns have different properties, so it is important to choose an appropriate blend for your project.

Synthetic fibres

Microfibre

With a quality of velvety softness, microfibre is increasingly common in multi-fibre yarns, as it is efficient at holding other fibres together as one yarn. Synthetic fibres such as this may not appeal to you, but they are often included in a yarn to reduce density, add texture, or to prevent excess spun fibre from migrating and pilling on the surface of a piece of crochet.

Acrylic

Acrylic fibres are produced from ethylene, which is derived from oil, and they are very cheap to manufacture. Acrylic yarn feels slightly rougher than other synthetics, and often comes in very bright and luminous shades. Robust and resistant to moths, acrylic yarn is ideal for toys, novelty items, and budget projects. The yarn tends to accumulate static electricity.

Nylon

Polyamide, or nylon, is an incredibly strong and lightweight fibre. Its elasticity makes it perfect for use in crocheted fabrics, and it is often used to reinforce yarn blends for items that may be subjected to heavy wear such as sock and darning yarns. Like other man-made fibres, nylon improves the washability of the fibres it is blended with by preventing shrinkage and felting.

Yarn blends

Wool and cotton mixes

The strength and softness of cotton adds smoothness, breathability, and washability to wool's very warm (and sometimes scratchy) qualities. The blend is great for those with sensitive skin and for babies. Cotton and wool absorb dye differently, which may lead to a stranded colour appearance in such blends. Wool sheds fewer hairs when mixed with a stabilizing plant fibre.

Synthetic-only mixes

Manufacturers can mix man-made, easily manipulated fibres to create a variety of textures such as furry eyelash yarns, soft and smooth babywear yarns, and rough aran substitutes. Although they do not hold much warmth in comparison to animal fibres, most synthetic-only blends can be washed at a high temperature and tumble-dried.

Natural and synthetic mixes

Man-made fibres are often blended with natural fibres to bring structure, strength, and washability; also to alter their appearance, such as to add a sheen. They help bind other yarns, such as mohair and wool, together and prevent shedding; they also prevent animal fibres shrinking. The strength of such blends makes them perfect for socks or gloves.

Multicoloured yarns

Variegated wool yarn
Two strands of different colours are twisted around each other in this super-bulky-weight yarn. Each strand changes from dark to light and back again along its length.

Variegated cotton yarn
Thin strands of different colours are twisted around a core yarn to create this multicoloured yarn.

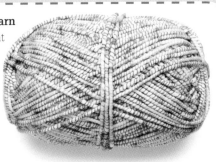

Novelty yarns and textural effects

Mohair
This fibre is the hair of a furry breed of goat, and it produces a unique natural "halo" when crocheted. Working with it can be challenging, as its fuzzy appearance makes it difficult to see the structure of the crochet and any mistakes made. Mohair makes particularly interesting oversized jumpers or accessories. It is not advisable to use mohair for babywear as it may shed hair when newly made, which could be dangerous if inhaled.

Bouclé yarn
The curly appearance of bouclé yarn results from whirls of fibre attached to a solid core yarn. When crocheted, these loops of fibre stand out and create a carpet-like looped fabric. (Bouclé is also the name of a type of fabric manufactured using a similarly spun yarn.) Bouclé yarns are completely unique and often specify a deceptively larger tension guideline as a result of their overall thickness. Bouclé is a lovely choice for very simply shaped garments.

Metallics
Although not a fibre, metallics are part of the library of yarns/fibres that is available to crocheters. Lurex and other metallic yarns make highly effective trims and decorations. They may be uncomfortable to wear if used on their own, but if blended with other yarns, they create very interesting mixes and are fun to experiment with.

Novelty yarn
Unique novelty yarns change with fashion trends. This shaggy yarn creates a crocheted fabric that looks like fur.

Buying yarn

Yarns are packaged for sale in specific quantities or "put-ups". The most common ones for crochet are balls, hanks, and skeins, which usually come in quantities of 25g, 50g, or 100g.

Preparing your yarn

DONUT

The stock in a yarn store may include balls that look like "donuts". These are ready to use: just pull the yarn from the centre to start crocheting.

CONE

This is often too heavy to carry around in a project bag and the yarn is best wound into balls before you start crocheting.

HANK

A twisted ring of yarn, also called a skein, which needs to be wound into a ball before it can be used. Do this by hand or with a ball-winder – you can check there are no knots or faults in the yarn as you wind it. Some yarns in hanks consist of delicate fibres, unsuitable for use in certain ball-winders.

BALL

A ball of yarn is ready to use without any special preparation. Keep the label in place as you work to ensure that the skein doesn't totally unravel.

Standard yarn-weight system

Yarn weight symbol & category names	**0** Lace	**1** Super fine	**2** Fine	**3** Light	**4** Medium	**5** Bulky	**6** Super bulky
Crochet tension ranges in dc to 10cm (4in)	32–42*** trebles	21–32 sts	16–20 sts	12–17 sts	11–14 sts	8–11 sts	5–9 sts
Recommended hook in metric size range	1.6–2.25mm	2.25–3.5mm	3.5–4.5mm	4.5–5.5mm	5.5–6.5mm	6.5–9mm	9mm and larger
Recommended hook in US size range	6 steel, 7 steel, 8 steel, B-1	B-1 to E-4	E-4 to 7	7 to I-9	I-9 to K-10½	K-10½ to M-13	M-13 and larger

GUIDELINES ONLY

The above reflect the most commonly used tensions and hook sizes for specific yarn categories. The categories of yarn, tension ranges, and recommended hook sizes have been devised by the Craft Yarn Council of America (YarnStandards.com).

*** Ultra-fine lace-weight yarns are difficult to put into tension ranges; always follow the tension given in your pattern for these yarns.

Defining yarn weight

Visual yarn thickness is only one indicator of a yarn-weight category. A yarn can look thicker than another yarn purely because of its loft, the air between the fibres, and the springiness of the strands. By stretching a strand you can see how much loft it has by how much the thickness diminishes. The ply of a yarn is also not an indication of yarn thickness. Plies are the strands spun together around each other to form the yarn. A yarn with four plies can be very thick or very thin depending on the thickness of each ply.

Yarn labels

Everything you need to know about a yarn is on its label. It will include symbols that tell you how to crochet with it and how to clean it. Here is just a selection of the most common symbols. Keep the labels so you can identify the dye-lot if you run short – you need to have the same dye-lot number as the original purchase to avoid a slight difference in colour in the finished item.

BALLBAND

A yarn label is also known as a ballband. It features information on the yarn's weight and thickness, as well as washing guidelines. Yarns range from the very fine and light to the thick, dense, and heavy.

SYMBOLS

Yarn manufacturers may use a system of symbols to give details of a yarn. These include descriptions of suitable hooks and the required tension.

Yarn weight and thickness

Recommended crochet hook size

Tension over a 10cm (4in) test square

Shade/colour number

Dye lot number

Weight of ball or skein

Fibre content

Machine-wash cold

Machine-wash cold, gentle cycle

Hand-wash cold

Hand-wash warm

Do not bleach

Dry-cleanable in any solvent

Dry-cleanable in certain solvents

Do not dry-clean

Do not tumble-dry

Do not iron

Iron on a low heat

Iron on a medium heat

Choosing yarn colours

When embarking on a new crochet project, the choice of colour is a very important decision. Even a simple design gains impact from good colour choices. The colour wheel is a useful tool, which will introduce you to colour theory. Colour has a visual "temperature", with some colours being perceived as "warm" and others as "cool". Colour temperature is an important element in whether a colour recedes or advances.

Colour wheel

The colour wheel: The three primary colours, red, yellow, and blue form the basis of a colour wheel. When two primary colours are combined, they create "secondaries". Red and yellow make orange, yellow and blue make green, and blue and red make purple. Intermediate colours called tertiaries occur when a secondary is mixed with the nearest primary.

Hue, shade, tone, and tint: Each segment shows the hue, shade, tone, and tint of a colour. A hue is the pure, bright colour; a shade is the colour mixed with black; a tone is the colour mixed with grey; and a tint is the colour mixed with white (pastels). The use of colour can affect the appearance of a project dramatically.

Complementary colours: Colours that lie opposite one another on the wheel, such as red and green, or yellow and violet, are called complementaries. They provide contrasts that accent design elements and make both colours stand out. Don't forget black and white, the ultimate opposites.

Monochromatic designs: These use different versions of the same colour. So a project based on greens will not stray into the red section of the colour wheel, but might have shades and tints of yellow and blue mixed in, which can then become "harmonious" combinations of colours that are next to each other on the colour wheel. These "adjacent" colours can also be combined to great effect, as long as there are differences in value between them.

Colour temperatures

WARM SHADES

The warm end of the colour spectrum consists mainly of red and yellow tones; browns, oranges, and purple are part of this group. Use these colours to bring richness and depth. A blend of warm shades can be a very flattering mixture to use, depending on your colouring: hold yarn against your face to see what suits you.

COOL SHADES

Blue, green, and violet are at the cool end of the spectrum, and these can look very good used together. Cool colours are generally darker in tone than warm ones. If used with warm shades, their impact is lessened: if you need to balance a warm mixture in a project, you will need a higher proportion of cool than warm colours to do it.

PASTELS

These very pale variations of darker colours are very popular for babies' and small children's garments; consequently, a variety of suitable synthetic yarns and blends is available. Pastels also feature strongly in spring/summer crochet patterns for adults: look for ice-cream colours in lightweight yarns, and enjoy using a delicate colour palette.

BRIGHTS

Vivid and fluorescent shades are fun to use in a project, and often make particularly eye-catching accessories or colour motifs. A great way to liven up a colourwork project that consists of muted shades is to add a bright edging or set of buttons. This burst of colour can change the project's overall impact completely.

Crochet tools

Crochet is probably one of the most economical needlework crafts as it requires very little equipment. If you are a beginner, start learning to crochet with a good-quality standard metal crochet hook. Once you know how to work the basic stitches with a lightweight wool yarn and a 4mm or 4.5mm (US size 6 or 7) hook, branch out and try some other types of hooks in order to find the one that suits you best.

Types of crochet hooks

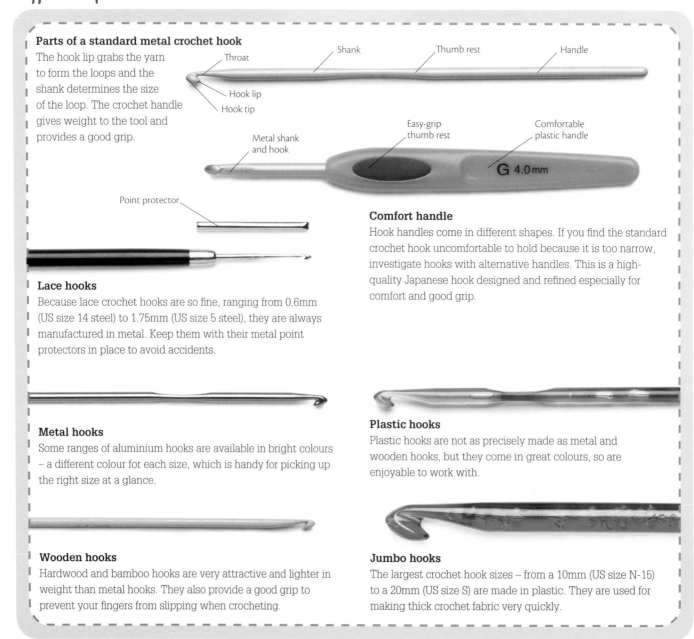

Parts of a standard metal crochet hook
The hook lip grabs the yarn to form the loops and the shank determines the size of the loop. The crochet handle gives weight to the tool and provides a good grip.

Throat

Shank

Thumb rest

Handle

Hook lip

Hook tip

Metal shank and hook

Easy-grip thumb rest

Comfortable plastic handle

G 4.0mm

Point protector

Comfort handle
Hook handles come in different shapes. If you find the standard crochet hook uncomfortable to hold because it is too narrow, investigate hooks with alternative handles. This is a high-quality Japanese hook designed and refined especially for comfort and good grip.

Lace hooks
Because lace crochet hooks are so fine, ranging from 0.6mm (US size 14 steel) to 1.75mm (US size 5 steel), they are always manufactured in metal. Keep them with their metal point protectors in place to avoid accidents.

Metal hooks
Some ranges of aluminium hooks are available in bright colours – a different colour for each size, which is handy for picking up the right size at a glance.

Plastic hooks
Plastic hooks are not as precisely made as metal and wooden hooks, but they come in great colours, so are enjoyable to work with.

Wooden hooks
Hardwood and bamboo hooks are very attractive and lighter in weight than metal hooks. They also provide a good grip to prevent your fingers from slipping when crocheting.

Jumbo hooks
The largest crochet hook sizes – from a 10mm (US size N-15) to a 20mm (US size S) are made in plastic. They are used for making thick crochet fabric very quickly.

Other equipment

CONVERSION CHART

This chart gives the conversions between the various hook-size systems. Where there are no exact conversions possible, use the nearest equivalent.

EU METRIC	US SIZES	OLD UK
0.6mm	14 steel	
0.75mm	12 steel	
1mm	11 steel	
1.25mm	7 steel	
1.5mm	6 steel	
1.75mm	5 steel	
2mm		14
2.25mm	B-1	
2.5mm		12
2.75mm	C-2	
3mm		10
3.25mm	D-3	
3.5mm	E-4	9
3.75mm	F-5	
4mm	G-6	8
4.5mm	7	7
5mm	H-8	6
5.5mm	I-9	5
6mm	J-10	4
6.5mm	K-10½	3
7mm		2
8mm	L-11	
9mm	M-13	
10mm	N-15	
12mm	P	
15mm	Q (16mm)	
20mm	S (19mm)	

In addition to a crochet hook, you will need a blunt-ended yarn needle for darning in yarn ends. Other essentials include pins, scissors, and a tape measure. Handy extras such as a row counter and stitch markers will help keep track of stitches.

Blunt-ended yarn needles
Use these for sewing seams and darning in yarn ends (make sure the eye of the needle is big enough for your chosen yarn).

Row counter
These are useful for keeping track of where you are in your crochet. String on a length of cotton yarn and hang it around your neck – change it each time you complete a row.

Stitch markers
These can be hooked onto the crochet to mark a specific row or a specific stitch in the row, or to mark the right-side of your crochet.

Pins
Use pins with glass heads or large heads (such as knitting pins), for blocking and seams (see pp.132–135).

Techniques and **projects**

Getting started

Before making your first loop, the slip knot (see p.24), get to know your hook and how to hold it. First, review the detailed explanation of the parts of the hook on p.18. Then try out the various hook- and yarn-holding techniques below and opposite when learning how to make chain stitches. If you ever learned crochet as a child, you will automatically hold the hook the way you originally learned to, and you should stick to this whether it is the pencil or knife position.

Holding the hook

Left-handed crocheters hold the hook in the exact mirror image of right-handed crocheters

Left-handed crocheters hold the hook in the exact mirror image of right-handed crocheters

5cm (2in)

5cm (2in)

Pencil position: To hold the hook in this position, grip it as you would a pencil. If the hook has a shaped thumb rest, position this above your thumb and under your forefinger. The centre of your thumb will be about 5cm (2in) from the tip of the hook if the hook has a thumb rest, and this is where you should also hold a hook without a thumb rest.

Knife position: To hold a crochet hook in this position, grip it as you would when using a table knife to cut food. As for the pencil position, if the hook has a thumb rest, settle your thumb and forefinger in this shaped section with the centre of your thumb about 5cm (2in) from the hook tip. Grip a hook without a thumb rest the same distance from the tip.

Holding the yarn

In order to control the flow of the yarn to your hook, you need to lace it around the fingers of your free hand (called your yarn hand). Both of the techniques shown here are only suggetions, so feel free to develop your own.

Method one: Start by winding the yarn around your little finger, then pass it under your two middle fingers and over your forefinger. With this method the forefinger is used to position the yarn.

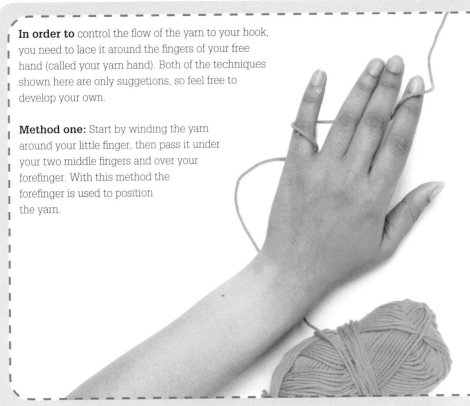

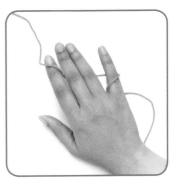

Left-handed crocheters thread the yarn through their right hand

Method two: Wrap the yarn around your little finger, then pass it behind the next finger and over the top of the middle finger and forefinger. This method allows you to position the yarn with either the forefinger or middle finger, whichever is more comfortable and gives you more control (see Tensioning your yarn on p.25).

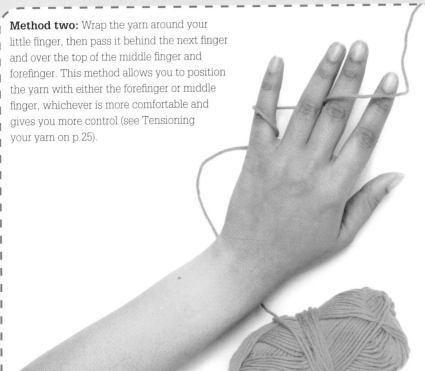

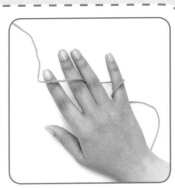

Left-handed crocheters thread the yarn through their right hand

Making a slip knot

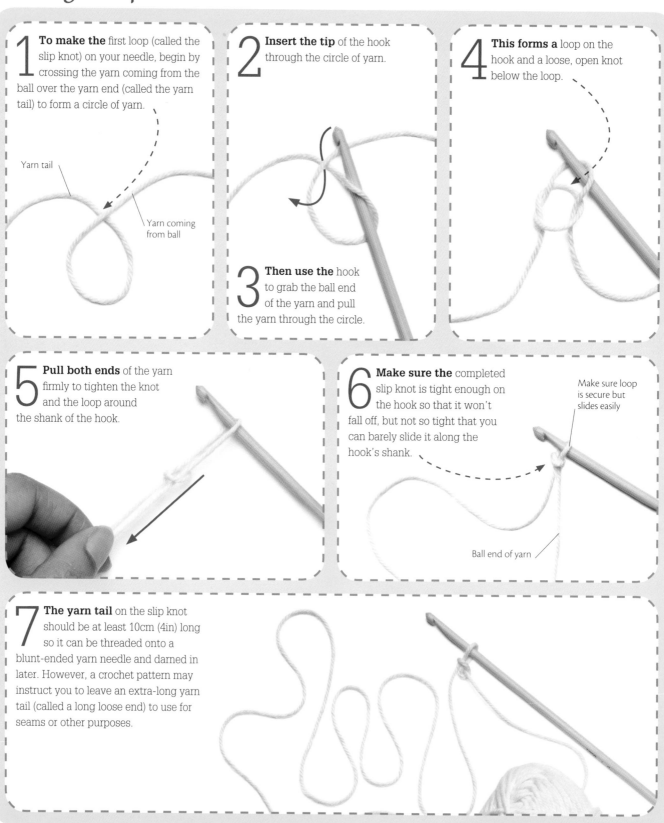

1 **To make the** first loop (called the slip knot) on your needle, begin by crossing the yarn coming from the ball over the yarn end (called the yarn tail) to form a circle of yarn.

Yarn tail

Yarn coming from ball

2 **Insert the tip** of the hook through the circle of yarn.

3 **Then use the** hook to grab the ball end of the yarn and pull the yarn through the circle.

4 **This forms a** loop on the hook and a loose, open knot below the loop.

5 **Pull both ends** of the yarn firmly to tighten the knot and the loop around the shank of the hook.

6 **Make sure the** completed slip knot is tight enough on the hook so that it won't fall off, but not so tight that you can barely slide it along the hook's shank.

Make sure loop is secure but slides easily

Ball end of yarn

7 **The yarn tail** on the slip knot should be at least 10cm (4in) long so it can be threaded onto a blunt-ended yarn needle and darned in later. However, a crochet pattern may instruct you to leave an extra-long yarn tail (called a long loose end) to use for seams or other purposes.

Tensioning your yarn

1 **With your slip** knot on your hook, try out some yarn-holding techniques. Wrap the yarn around your little finger and then lace it through your other fingers as desired, but so that it ends up over the tip of your forefinger (or your forefinger and middle finger).

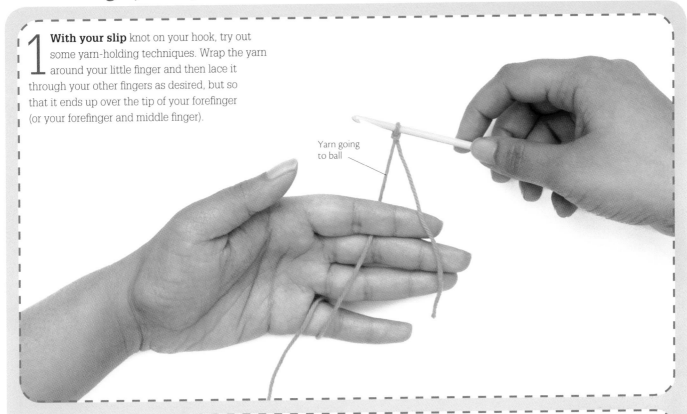

Yarn going to ball

2 **As you crochet,** grip the yarn tightly with your little finger and ring finger and release it gently as you form the loops. Use either your forefinger or your middle finger to position the yarn, and hold the base of the crochet close to the hook to keep it in place as the hook is drawn through the loops.

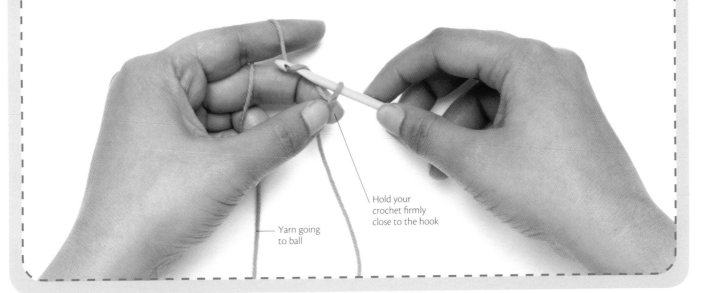

Hold your crochet firmly close to the hook

Yarn going to ball

Chain stitches

Chain stitches are the first crochet stitches you need to learn because they form the base for all other stitches – called a foundation chain – and for turning chains (see p.30). They are used in combination with other basic stitches to create a vast array of crochet stitch patterns, both densely textured stitches and lacy ones. Practise chain stitches until you are comfortable holding a hook and releasing and tensioning yarn.

Making a foundation chain

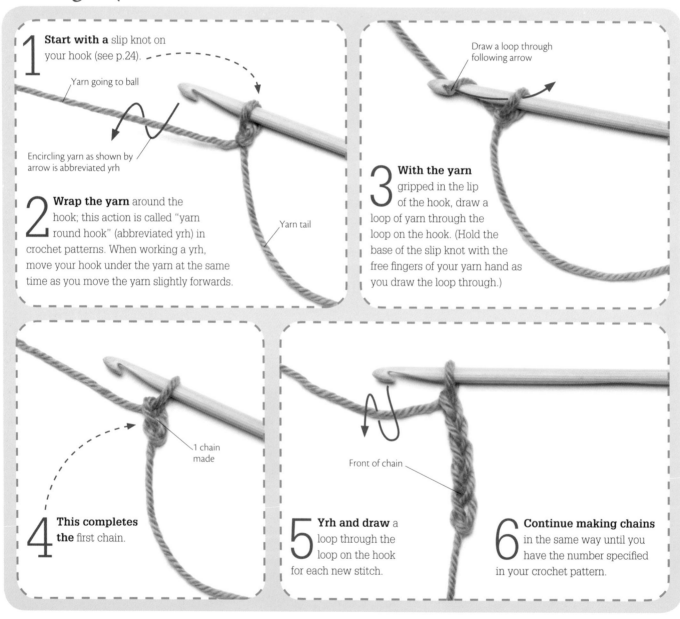

1 **Start with a** slip knot on your hook (see p.24).

Yarn going to ball

Encircling yarn as shown by arrow is abbreviated yrh

2 **Wrap the yarn** around the hook; this action is called "yarn round hook" (abbreviated yrh) in crochet patterns. When working a yrh, move your hook under the yarn at the same time as you move the yarn slightly forwards.

Yarn tail

Draw a loop through following arrow

3 **With the yarn** gripped in the lip of the hook, draw a loop of yarn through the loop on the hook. (Hold the base of the slip knot with the free fingers of your yarn hand as you draw the loop through.)

4 **This completes the** first chain.

1 chain made

5 **Yrh and draw a** loop through the loop on the hook for each new stitch.

Front of chain

6 **Continue making chains** in the same way until you have the number specified in your crochet pattern.

Counting chain stitches

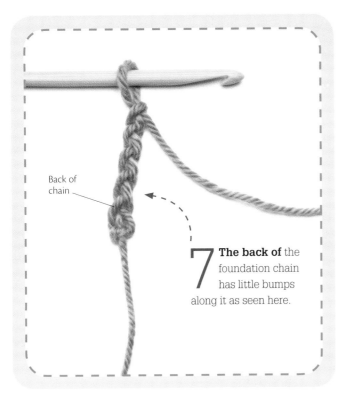

Back of chain

7 **The back of** the foundation chain has little bumps along it as seen here.

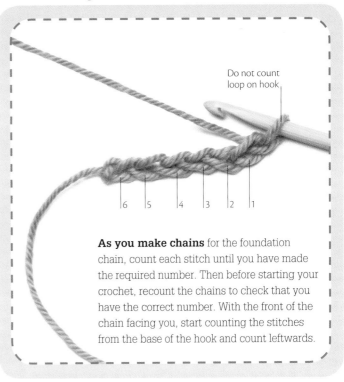

Do not count loop on hook

6 5 4 3 2 1

As you make chains for the foundation chain, count each stitch until you have made the required number. Then before starting your crochet, recount the chains to check that you have the correct number. With the front of the chain facing you, start counting the stitches from the base of the hook and count leftwards.

Simple chain stitch necklace

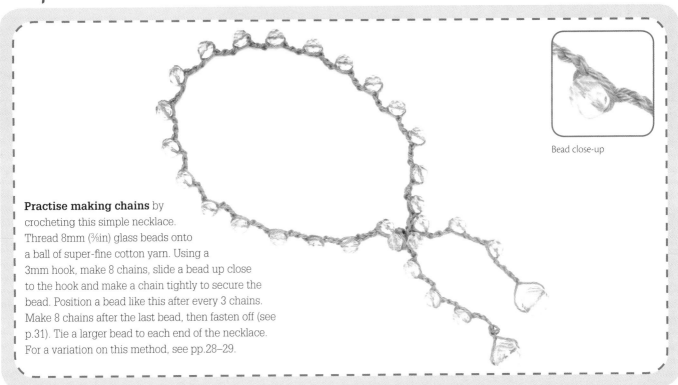

Bead close-up

Practise making chains by crocheting this simple necklace. Thread 8mm (⅜in) glass beads onto a ball of super-fine cotton yarn. Using a 3mm hook, make 8 chains, slide a bead up close to the hook and make a chain tightly to secure the bead. Position a bead like this after every 3 chains. Make 8 chains after the last bead, then fasten off (see p.31). Tie a larger bead to each end of the necklace. For a variation on this method, see pp.28–29.

Bead necklace

This beautiful necklace is a great crochet project for beginners as it uses just one stitch – the chain stitch (see pages 26–27).

essential info ...

SIZE
One size fits all

YARN
A: Scrap of Rowan Siena 4-ply

A

CROCHET HOOK
2mm hook
1mm hook (if needed)

NOTIONS
Approximately 15 beads in different sizes and shapes (ensure the holes are large enough for the beads to pass easily over at least a 1mm crochet hook)
Yarn needle

Necklace
Work 10 ch.

Thread a bead onto the hook and insert it back through the loop. Pass the bead onto the loop, pulling the loop through it. If necessary, use a 1mm hook for this step.

If you switched hooks, return to the 2mm hook, yo, pull the yarn through the loop to secure the bead in place.

Cont chaining and adding beads in this way, until the necklace is the length you require.

Finishing
Ss in the first chain to join the necklace ends. Cut the yarn, leaving a tail. Pass the tail through the last loop and tighten to finish off. Using a yarn needle, work both yarn tails through the chains on either side of the last ss.

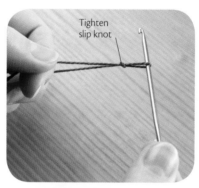

Tighten slip knot

tips ...

Make a slip knot to start by first crossing the yarn coming from the ball over itself to form a circle. Insert the 2mm hook through the circle and pull the ball end through the circle. Tighten.

To secure the bead, grasp the yarn coming through the ball with the tip of the hook, then pull the yarn through the loop.

Make two necklaces, one slightly shorter than the other, so that you can ring the changes.

Use a variety of shapes, size, and colour of beads and thread them on in a strict order or go for a more informal random look.

Beginner's tips

Slip stitches are the shortest of all the crochet stitches. Although they can be worked in rows, the resulting fabric is so dense that it is only really suitable for bag handles. However, slip stitches appear very frequently in crochet instructions – to join on new yarn (see p.33), to work invisibly along the top of a row to move to a new position (see p.85), and to join rounds in circular crochet (see p.100).

Working slip stitch as a fabric (abbreviation = ss)

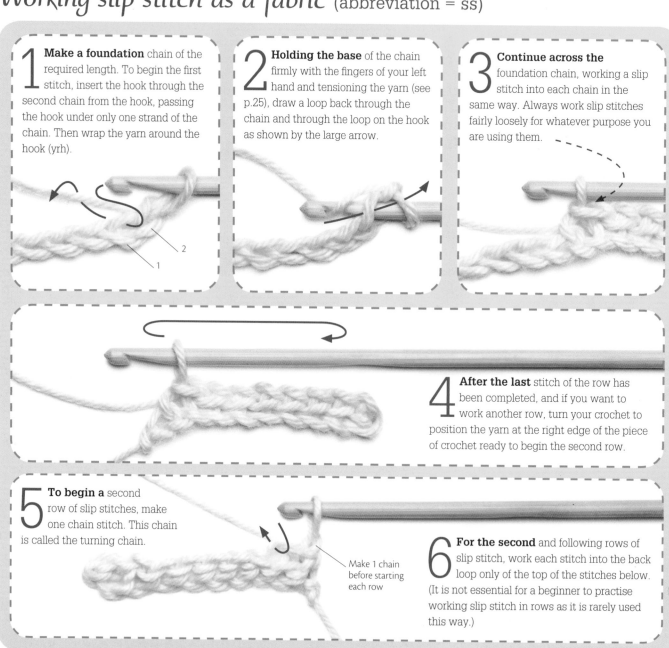

1 **Make a foundation** chain of the required length. To begin the first stitch, insert the hook through the second chain from the hook, passing the hook under only one strand of the chain. Then wrap the yarn around the hook (yrh).

2 **Holding the base** of the chain firmly with the fingers of your left hand and tensioning the yarn (see p.25), draw a loop back through the chain and through the loop on the hook as shown by the large arrow.

3 **Continue across the** foundation chain, working a slip stitch into each chain in the same way. Always work slip stitches fairly loosely for whatever purpose you are using them.

4 **After the last** stitch of the row has been completed, and if you want to work another row, turn your crochet to position the yarn at the right edge of the piece of crochet ready to begin the second row.

5 **To begin a** second row of slip stitches, make one chain stitch. This chain is called the turning chain.

Make 1 chain before starting each row

6 **For the second** and following rows of slip stitch, work each stitch into the back loop only of the top of the stitches below. (It is not essential for a beginner to practise working slip stitch in rows as it is rarely used this way.)

Using slip stitches to form a foundation ring

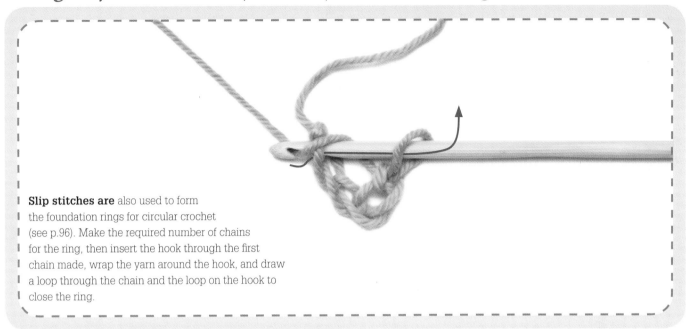

Slip stitches are also used to form the foundation rings for circular crochet (see p.96). Make the required number of chains for the ring, then insert the hook through the first chain made, wrap the yarn around the hook, and draw a loop through the chain and the loop on the hook to close the ring.

Fastening off a length of chains

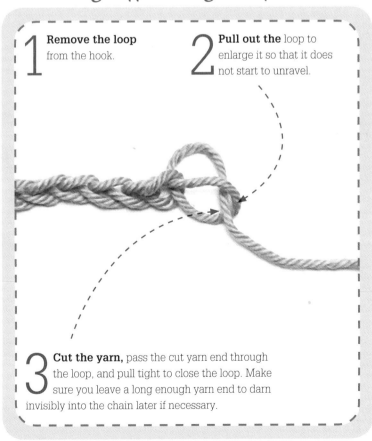

1 **Remove the loop** from the hook.

2 **Pull out the** loop to enlarge it so that it does not start to unravel.

3 **Cut the yarn,** pass the cut yarn end through the loop, and pull tight to close the loop. Make sure you leave a long enough yarn end to darn invisibly into the chain later if necessary.

Fastening off slip stitches

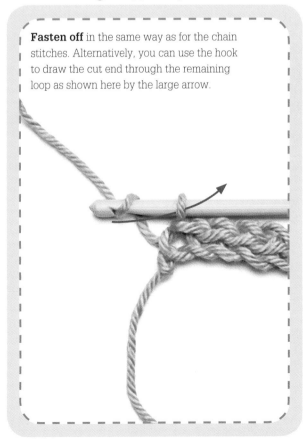

Fasten off in the same way as for the chain stitches. Alternatively, you can use the hook to draw the cut end through the remaining loop as shown here by the large arrow.

Joining on new yarn

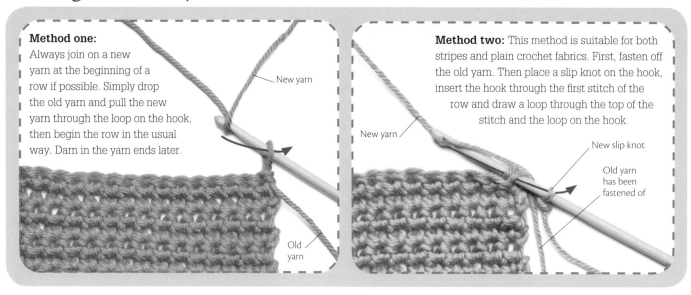

Method one:
Always join on a new yarn at the beginning of a row if possible. Simply drop the old yarn and pull the new yarn through the loop on the hook, then begin the row in the usual way. Darn in the yarn ends later.

New yarn

Old yarn

Method two: This method is suitable for both stripes and plain crochet fabrics. First, fasten off the old yarn. Then place a slip knot on the hook, insert the hook through the first stitch of the row and draw a loop through the top of the stitch and the loop on the hook.

New yarn

New slip knot

Old yarn has been fastened of

Darning in yarn

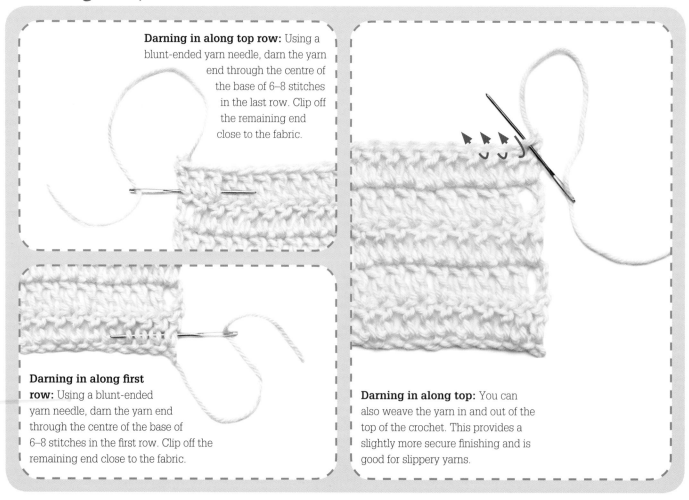

Darning in along top row: Using a blunt-ended yarn needle, darn the yarn end through the centre of the base of 6–8 stitches in the last row. Clip off the remaining end close to the fabric.

Darning in along first row: Using a blunt-ended yarn needle, darn the yarn end through the centre of the base of 6–8 stitches in the first row. Clip off the remaining end close to the fabric.

Darning in along top: You can also weave the yarn in and out of the top of the crochet. This provides a slightly more secure finishing and is good for slippery yarns.

Counting crochet stitches

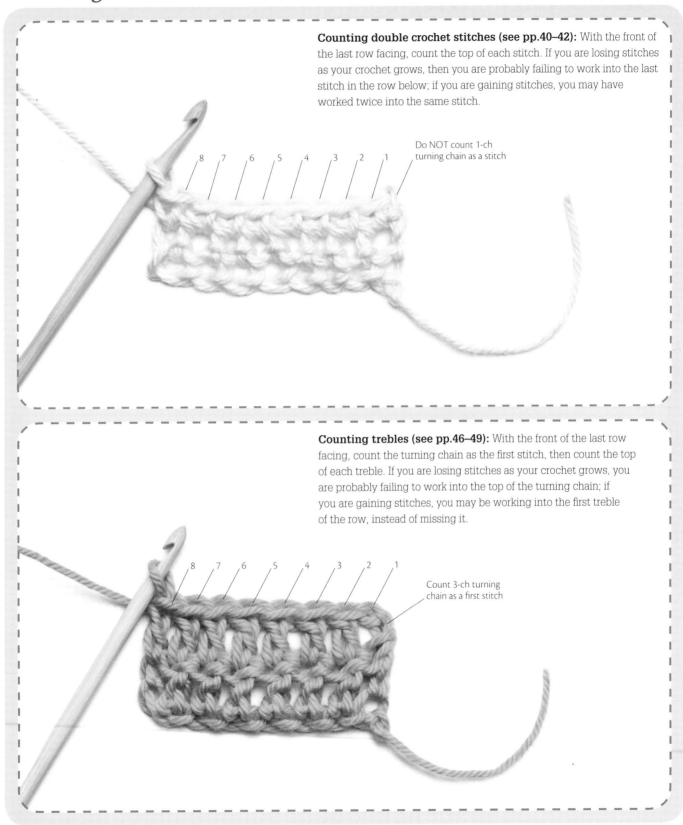

Counting double crochet stitches (see pp.40–42): With the front of the last row facing, count the top of each stitch. If you are losing stitches as your crochet grows, then you are probably failing to work into the last stitch in the row below; if you are gaining stitches, you may have worked twice into the same stitch.

8 7 6 5 4 3 2 1

Do NOT count 1-ch turning chain as a stitch

Counting trebles (see pp.46–49): With the front of the last row facing, count the turning chain as the first stitch, then count the top of each treble. If you are losing stitches as your crochet grows, you are probably failing to work into the top of the turning chain; if you are gaining stitches, you may be working into the first treble of the row, instead of missing it.

8 7 6 5 4 3 2 1

Count 3-ch turning chain as a first stitch

Following simple stitch patterns

Working a project from a crochet pattern for the first time can seem difficult for a beginner, especially if an experienced crocheter is not at hand to offer help. The best way to prepare for a crochet pattern is to first practise crocheting rectangles of various stitch patterns using simple stitch techniques. This is a good introduction to following abbreviated written row instructions.

Understanding written instructions

As long as you know how to work all the basic stitches on pp.40–57 and have reviewed pp.58–63 and 66–67, where special stitch techniques are explained, there is nothing stopping you from working the projects on pp.38–39, 50–53, and 62–69. Simply consult the lists below and opposite for the meanings of the various abbreviations and follow the written row instructions one step at a time.

Begin by making the required number of chains for the foundation chain, using your chosen yarn and one of the hook sizes recommended for the yarn weight on pp.14–15. Crochet a swatch that repeats the pattern only a few times to test it out.

(If you decide to make a blanket or cushion cover with the stitch later, you can adjust the hook size before starting it to obtain the exact flexibility of fabric you desire.)

Work each row of the stitch pattern slowly and mark the right side of the fabric (if there is one) as soon as you start, by tying a contrasting coloured thread to it. Another good tip is to tick off the rows as you complete them or put a sticky note under them so you don't lose your place in the pattern. If you do get lost in all the stitches, pull out all the rows and start from the foundation chain again.

Crochet terminology

The following terms are commonly used in crochet patterns. Many crochet terms are the same in the UK and the US, but where they differ, the US equivalent is given in parentheses. Turn to the pages indicated for how to work the various increases, decreases, or stitch techniques listed.

bobble: Several stitches worked into the same stitch in the row below and joined together at the top (see p.77).

cluster: Several stitches worked into different stitches in the row below, but joined together at the top (see p.76).

dc2tog (work 2 dc together): See p.83. (US sc2tog)

dc3tog (work 3 dc together): [Insert hook in next st, yrh and draw a loop through] 3 times, yrh and draw through all 4 loops on hook – 2 sts decreased. (US sc3tog)

facing: Facing toward you as you're working.

fasten off: Cut the yarn and draw the yarn tail through the remaining loop on the hook (see p.31).

foundation chain: The base of chain stitches that the first row of crochet is worked onto (see pp.26–27).

foundation row: The first row of a piece of crochet (the row worked onto the foundation chain) is sometimes called the foundation row.

htr2tog (work 2 htr together): [Yrh and insert hook in next st, yrh and draw a loop through] twice, yrh and draw through all 5 loops on hook – 1 st decreased. (US hdc2tog)

htr3tog (work 3 htr together): [Yrh and insert hook in next st, yrh and draw a loop through] 3 times, yrh and draw through all 7 loops on hook – 2 sts decreased. (US hdc3tog)

miss a stitch: Do not work into the stitch, but go on to the next stitch. (US "skip" a stitch)

shell: Several stitches worked into the same stitch in the previous row or into the same chain space (see p.61).

pineapple: A bobble made with half trebles; also called a puff stitch.

popcorn: A type of bobble.

puff stitch: See pineapple.

tr2tog (work 2 tr together): See pp.84–85. (US dc2tog)

tr3tog (work 3 tr together): [Yrh and insert hook in next st, yrh and draw a loop through, yrh and draw through first 2 loops on hook] 3 times, yrh and draw through all 4 loops on hook – 2 sts decreased. (US dc3tog)

turning chain: The chain/s worked at the beginning of the row (or round) to bring the hook up to the correct height for working the following stitches in the row (see p.30).

Crochet abbreviations

These are the abbreviations most commonly used in crochet patterns. The abbreviations for the basic stitches are listed first and the other abbreviations found in crochet patterns follow. Any special abbreviations in a crochet pattern will always be explained in the pattern.

ABBREVIATIONS FOR BASIC STITCHES

Note: The names for the basic crochet stitches differ in the UK and the US. This book uses UK crochet terminology, so if you have learned to crochet in the US, be sure to take note of the difference in terminology.

ch	chain
ss	slip stitch
dc	double crochet (US single crochet – sc)
htr	half treble (US half double crochet – hdc)
tr	treble (US double crochet – dc)
dtr	double treble (US treble crochet – tr)
trtr	triple treble (US double treble crochet – dtr)
qtr	quadruple treble (US triple treble crochet – trtr)
quintr	quintuple treble (US quadruple treble – quadtr)

OTHER ABBREVIATIONS

alt	alternate
beg	begin(ning)
cm	centimetre(s)
cont	continu(e)(ing)
dc2tog	see Crochet terminology
dc3tog	see Crochet Terminology
dec	decreas(e)(ing)
foll	follow(s)(ing)
g	gram(s)
htr2tog	see Crochet Terminology
htr3tog	see Crochet Terminology
in	inch(es)
inc	increas(e)(ing)
m	metre(s)
mm	millimetre(s)
oz	ounce(s)
patt(s)	pattern(s)
rem	remain(s)(ing)

rep	repeat(s)(ing)
RS	right side
sp	space(s)
st(s)	stitch(es)
TBL	through back loop
TFL	through front loop
tog	together
tr2tog	see Crochet Terminology
tr3tog	see Crochet Terminology
WS	wrong side
yd	yard(s)
yrh	yarn round hook (US yarn over hook – yo)
*	Repeat instructions after asterisk or between asterisks as many times as instructed.
[ ]	Repeat instructions inside square brackets as many times as instructed.

Following a crochet pattern

Followed step by step and slowly, crochet patterns are not as difficult to understand as they appear. The guides here give many tips for how to approach your first crochet patterns.

Simple accessory patterns

A beginner should choose an easy accessory pattern for a first crochet project. A striped cushion cover is given here as an example. Follow the numbered tips of the guide to familiarize yourself with the parts of a simple pattern.

1 The skill level required for the crochet is given at the beginning of most patterns. In this book, all the patterns are easy. When starting out, work several easy patterns before progressing to the intermediate level.

2 Check the size of the finished item. If it is a simple square like this cushion, you can easily adjust the size by adding or subtracting stitches and rows.

3 It is sometimes advisable to use the yarn specified. But if you are unable to obtain this yarn, choose a substitute yarn.

8 Make a tension swatch before starting to crochet and change the hook size if necessary (see p.37).

9 Instructions for working a piece of crocheted fabric always start with how many chains to make for the foundation chain and which yarn or hook size to use. If there is only one hook size and one yarn, these may be absent here.

10 Consult the abbreviations list with your pattern for the meanings of abbreviations (see p.35).

13 Fastening off completes the crochet piece.

14 The back of a cushion cover is sometimes exactly the same as the front or it may have a fabric back. In this example, the stripes are reversed on the back for a more versatile cover.

15 After all the crocheted pieces are completed, follow the Finishing (or Making Up) section of the pattern.

16 See p.32 for how to darn in loose ends.

Striped cushion cover

SKILLS LEVEL
Easy

SIZE OF FINISHED CUSHION
40.5cm x 40.5cm (16in x 16in)

MATERIALS
7 x 25g/⅞oz (110m/120yd) balls of branded Scottish Tweed 4-Ply in Thatch 00018 (**A**) 4 x 25g/⅞oz (110m/120yd) balls of branded Scottish Tweed 4-Ply in Skye 00009 (**B**) 3.5mm (US size E-4) crochet hook
Cushion pad to fit finished cover

TENSION
22 sts and 24 rows to 10cm (4in) over double crochet using 3.5mm (US size E-4) hook or size necessary to achieve correct tension. To save time, take time to check tension.

FRONT
Using 3.5mm (US size E-4) hook and A, make 89 ch.
Row 1: 1 dc in 2nd ch from hook, 1 dc in each of rem ch, turn. 88 dc.
Row 2: 1 ch (does NOT count as a st), 1 dc in each dc to end, turn.
Rep row 2 throughout to form dc fabric.
Always changing to new colour with last yrh of last dc of previous row, work in stripes as follows:
26 rows more in A, 8 rows B, [8 rows A, 8 rows B] twice, 28 rows A.
Fasten off.

BACK
Work as for Front, but use B for A, and A for B.

Finishing
Darn in loose ends.
Block and press lightly on wrong side, following instructions on yarn label.
With wrong sides facing, sew three sides of back and front together. Turn right-side out, insert cushion pad, and sew remaining seam.

4 Always purchase the same total amount in metres/yards of a substitute yarn; NOT the same amount in weight.

5 If desired, select different colours to suit your décor; the colours specified are just suggestions.

6 Alter the hook size if you cannot achieve the correct tension with the specified size (see 8 left).

7 Extra items needed for your project will usually be listed under Materials, Extras, or Notions.

11 Work in the specified stitch pattern, for the specified number of rows or cm/in.

12 Colours for stripes are always changed at the end of the previous row before the colour change so the first turning chain of the new stripe is in the correct colour (see p.70).

17 Make sure you look at the yarn label instructions before attempting to press any piece of crochet. The label may say that the yarn cannot be pressed or it can be pressed only with a cool iron. (See p.132 for blocking tips.)

18 See pp.133–135 for seaming options. Take time with seams on crochet, and when working your very first seams, get an experienced crocheter to help you.

Garment patterns

Garment instructions usually start with the Skill Level, followed by the Sizes, Materials, Tension, and finally the Instructions. Most important for successfully making a garment – or other fitted items such as hats, mittens, gloves, and socks – is choosing the right size and making a tension swatch. Follow the tips here to help you get the most out of a pattern.

Choose a skill level that suits your crochet experience. If in doubt or if you haven't crocheted for many years, stick to an Easy or Beginner's level until you are confident you can go to the next level.

White is a good colour to use for your first crocheted sweater because the stitches are so easy to see clearly. But if you do choose white yarn, be sure to wash your hands every time you start crocheting; and when you stop, put away the yarn and sweater in a bag to keep it from becoming soiled.

Avoid black or other very dark yarn for a first crocheted sweater as the stitches are very difficult to distinguish, even for an accomplished crocheter.

Purchase yarn balls that have the same dye-lot number (see p.15).

Have a set of hook sizes at hand if you are starting to crochet sweaters. When checking tension (see below), you may need other hook sizes in order to achieve the correct tension.

Always make the pieces in the order given in the instructions, whether you are crocheting a garment, accessory, or toy. On a garment, the back is usually crocheted first, followed by the front, and lastly the sleeves. Pockets that are integrated into the fronts are crocheted before the fronts and those applied as patches are worked last.

Beginners should take care when modifying patterns as sizing/shaping and stitch patterns are often worked out in detail by the pattern designer and may turn out very differently if altered. However, beginners should not be afraid to try modifying a pattern to suit their preferences, as it can always be pulled back if it does not work as planned.

Measuring tension

It is essential to check your tension (stitch size) before beginning a crochet pattern if the final size of the piece matters. Not everyone crochets stitches with exactly the same tightness or looseness, so you may well need to use a different hook size to achieve the stitch size required by your pattern.

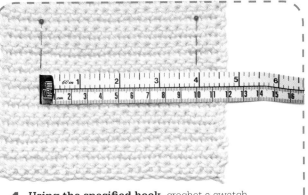

1 **Using the specified hook,** crochet a swatch about 13cm (5in) square. Mark 10cm (4in) across the centre with pins and count the number of stitches between the pins.

2 **Count the number** of rows to 10cm (4in) in the same way. If you have fewer stitches and rows than you should try again with a smaller hook size; if you have more, change to a larger hook size. Use the hook size that best matches the correct tension. (Matching the stitch width is much more important than matching the row height.)

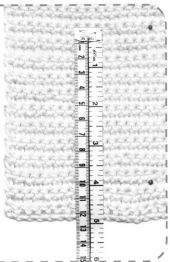

Crowls

These crocheted owls or "Crowls" are made from a strip of crochet using only double crochet (see pp.40–42). They make cute little soft toys and even a useful addition to your sewing kit – see the variation opposite, top.

Small owl body
Using orange yarn, work 10 ch.

Row 1: Make 1 ch, dc in 2nd chain from hook, 1 dc in each ch to end. Turn. Cont in dc until work measures 18cm (7in) and fasten off.

OWL EYES
Using blue yarn, work 2 ch. Dc 10 times into the first ch, ss into the first dc.

Fasten off, weave in all ends.

Finishing
Sew in the loose ends, then fold the strip in half and stitch the sides together. Turn the work inside out and stuff the toy, but don't overfill it. Stitch the bottom edge to close the hole and then sew the eyes in place. For the owl's nose, lightly stitch a triangular scrap of green felt between the eyes.

The best technique to use for neatly stitching the sides together is overcast stitch (see p.133).

tips ...

To close the hole, sew running stitch around the opening, then pull the thread to gather up the crochet and close the hole.

When sewing the eyes onto the crowls, use thread that matches the eyes rather than the body and stitch all around the edge of the crochet circles.

Instead of stuffing the small owl you can turn it into a handy tape-measure holder. Just pop the tape measure inside and lightly stitch up the opening, checking that the tape measure can run freely in and out.

Large owl body
To make the large owl body, work as for the small owl, but work 16 ch and continue as given until the work measures 26cm (10in). Fasten off.

Double crochet

Double crochet is the easiest crochet stitch to learn and one crocheters use frequently, either on its own or in combination with other stitches. Take your time learning and practising the stitch because once you become proficient, the taller stitches will be much easier to master. Double crochet forms a dense fabric that is suitable for many types of garments and accessories. It is also the stitch used for toys and containers because it can be worked tightly to form a stiff, firm textile.

Working double crochet stitch (abbreviation = dc)

When double crochet is worked back and forth in rows, it looks identical on both sides. Worked in the round it looks different on the right and wrong sides, which you can see on p.105.

1 **Make a foundation** chain of the required length (see pp.26–27).

2 **Insert the hook** through the second stitch from the hook and wrap the yarn around the hook (yrh) following the large arrow. (You can insert the hook under one or two strands of the chain, but working under just one loop as shown here is easiest.)

3 Holding the base of the chain firmly with your left hand and tensioning the yarn (see p.25), draw a loop back through the chain, as shown by the large arrow.

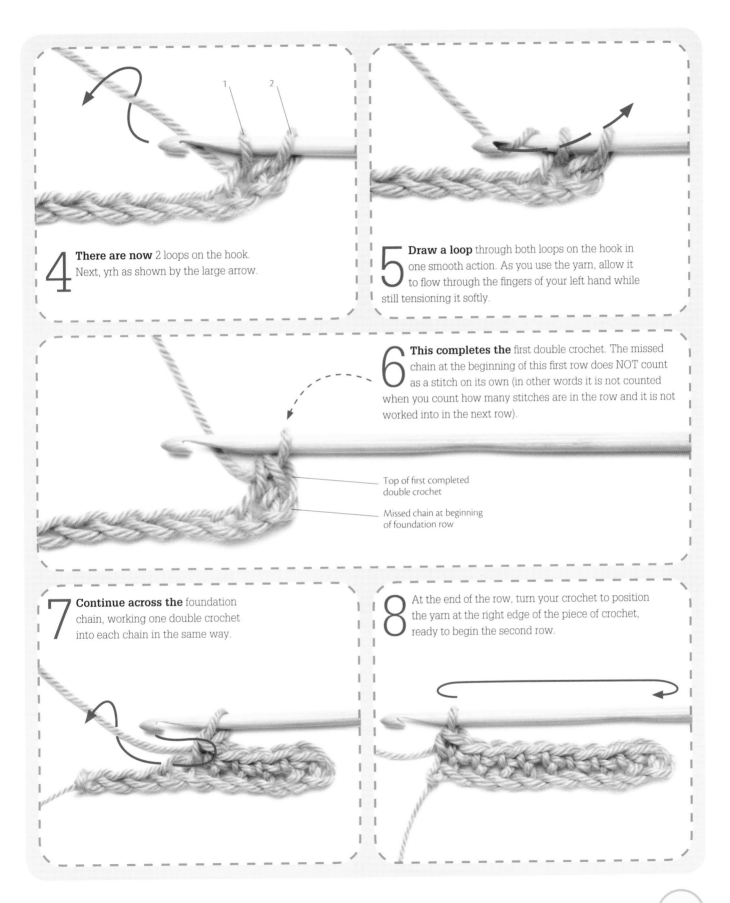

4 **There are now** 2 loops on the hook. Next, yrh as shown by the large arrow.

5 **Draw a loop** through both loops on the hook in one smooth action. As you use the yarn, allow it to flow through the fingers of your left hand while still tensioning it softly.

6 **This completes the** first double crochet. The missed chain at the beginning of this first row does NOT count as a stitch on its own (in other words it is not counted when you count how many stitches are in the row and it is not worked into in the next row).

Top of first completed double crochet

Missed chain at beginning of foundation row

7 **Continue across the** foundation chain, working one double crochet into each chain in the same way.

8 At the end of the row, turn your crochet to position the yarn at the right edge of the piece of crochet, ready to begin the second row.

9 **To begin the** second row, make one chain stitch. This chain is called the turning chain, and it brings the work up to the height of the double crochet stitches that will follow.

1-chain turning chain does NOT count as first stitch of row

10 Work the first double crochet into the top of the first stitch in the row below. Be sure to insert the hook under both legs of the "V" of the stitch. Work a double crochet into the top of each of the remaining double crochets in the row below.

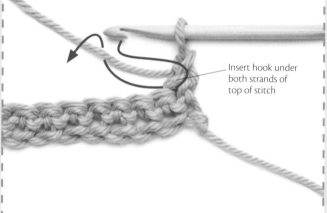

Insert hook under both strands of top of stitch

11 At the end of the row, work the last stitch into the top of the last double crochet of the row below. Work following rows as for the second row.

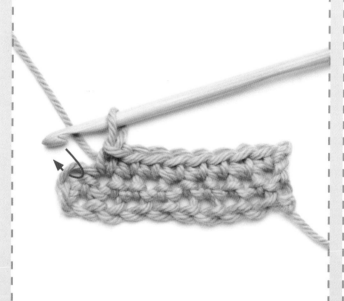

12 When you have completed your crochet, cut the yarn leaving a long loose end – at least 10cm (4in) long.

13 Remove the hook from the remaining loop, pass the yarn end through the loop, and pull tight to close it. Fastening off like this is done the same way for all crochet stitches.

Half treble crochet

After double crochet, half treble crochet comes next in order of stitch heights. It is firm like double crochet and fairly dense, but produces a slightly softer texture, which makes it ideal for making warm baby garments. It's not advisable to move on to learning how to work half trebles until you can make double crochet stitches with confidence (see pp. 40–42).

Working half treble stitch (abbreviation = htr)

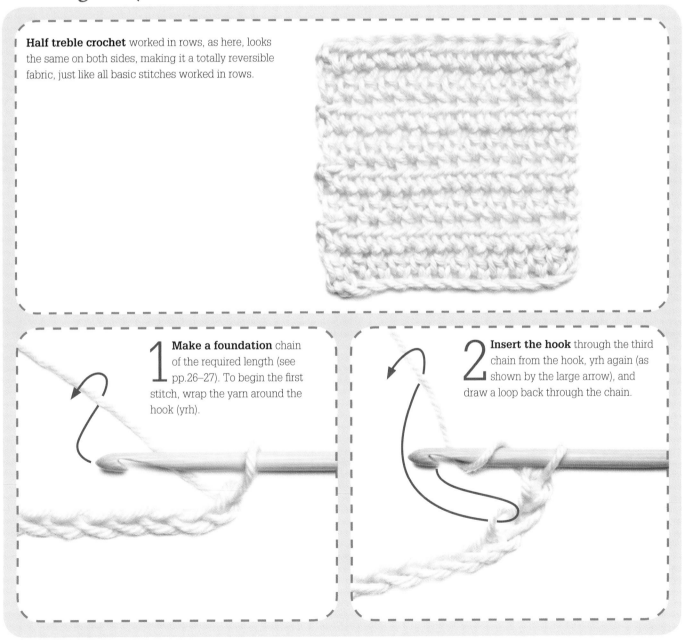

Half treble crochet worked in rows, as here, looks the same on both sides, making it a totally reversible fabric, just like all basic stitches worked in rows.

1 **Make a foundation** chain of the required length (see pp.26–27). To begin the first stitch, wrap the yarn around the hook (yrh).

2 **Insert the hook** through the third chain from the hook, yrh again (as shown by the large arrow), and draw a loop back through the chain.

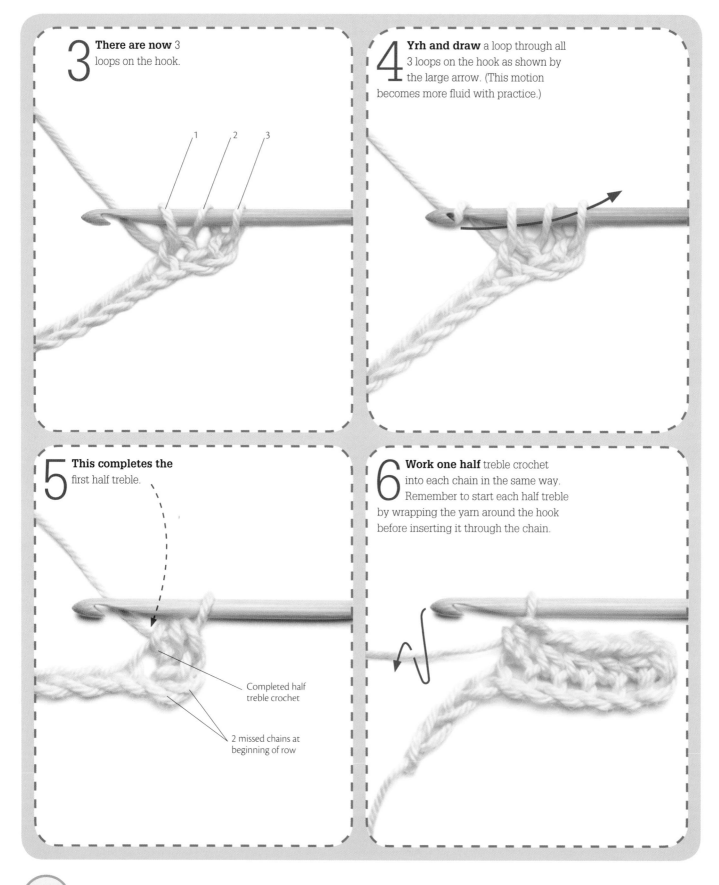

3 **There are now** 3 loops on the hook.

1 2 3

4 **Yrh and draw** a loop through all 3 loops on the hook as shown by the large arrow. (This motion becomes more fluid with practice.)

5 **This completes the** first half treble.

Completed half treble crochet

2 missed chains at beginning of row

6 **Work one half** treble crochet into each chain in the same way. Remember to start each half treble by wrapping the yarn around the hook before inserting it through the chain.

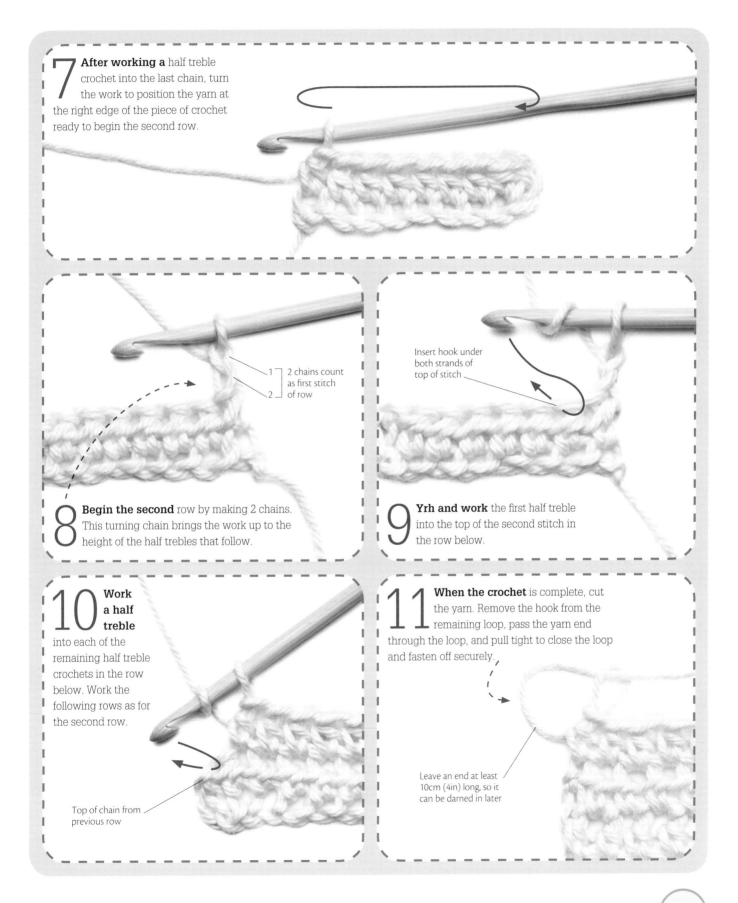

7 **After working a** half treble crochet into the last chain, turn the work to position the yarn at the right edge of the piece of crochet ready to begin the second row.

8 **Begin the second** row by making 2 chains. This turning chain brings the work up to the height of the half trebles that follow.

1 ⎤
2 ⎦ 2 chains count as first stitch of row

9 **Yrh and work** the first half treble into the top of the second stitch in the row below.

Insert hook under both strands of top of stitch

10 **Work a half treble** into each of the remaining half treble crochets in the row below. Work the following rows as for the second row.

Top of chain from previous row

11 **When the crochet** is complete, cut the yarn. Remove the hook from the remaining loop, pass the yarn end through the loop, and pull tight to close the loop and fasten off securely.

Leave an end at least 10cm (4in) long, so it can be darned in later

Treble crochet

Treble crochet produces a more open and softer crochet fabric than the denser double and half treble crochet. Because treble crochet is a tall stitch, the fabric grows quickly as you proceed, which makes it the most popular of all crochet stitches.

Working treble stitch (abbreviation = tr)

As you work treble crochet in rows, you will see that it looks identical on the front and the back.

1 **Make as many** chains as required (see p.26). To begin the first stitch, wrap the yarn around the hook (yrh).

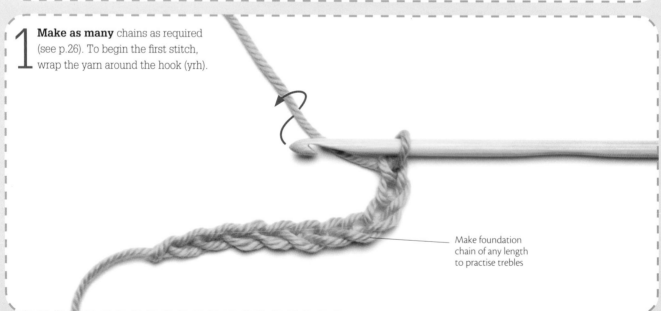

Make foundation chain of any length to practise trebles

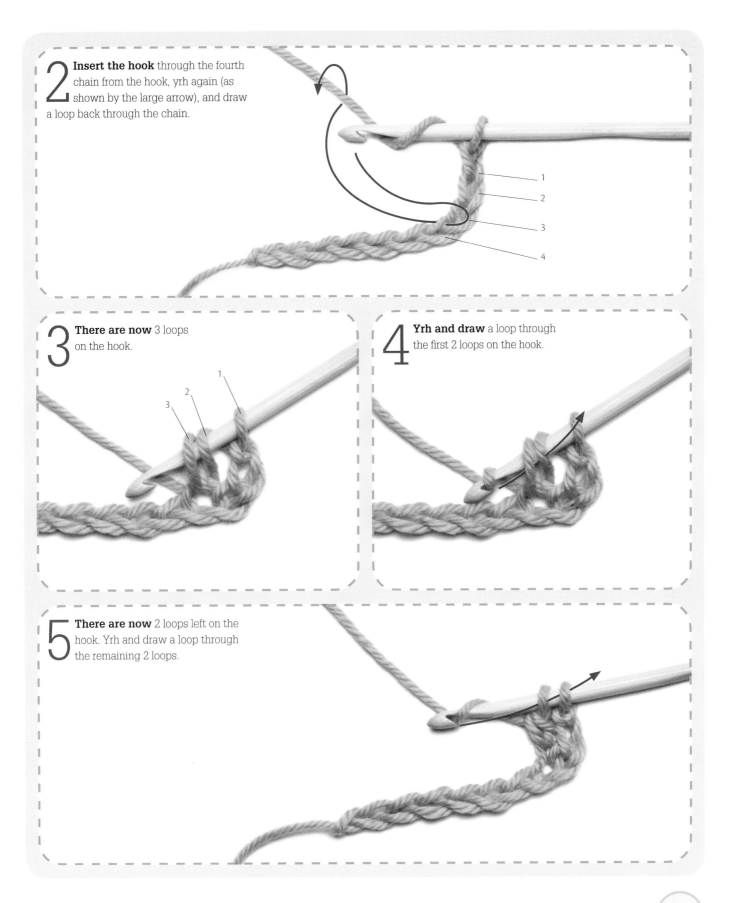

2 **Insert the hook** through the fourth chain from the hook, yrh again (as shown by the large arrow), and draw a loop back through the chain.

1
2
3
4

3 **There are now** 3 loops on the hook.

1
2
3

4 **Yrh and draw** a loop through the first 2 loops on the hook.

5 **There are now** 2 loops left on the hook. Yrh and draw a loop through the remaining 2 loops.

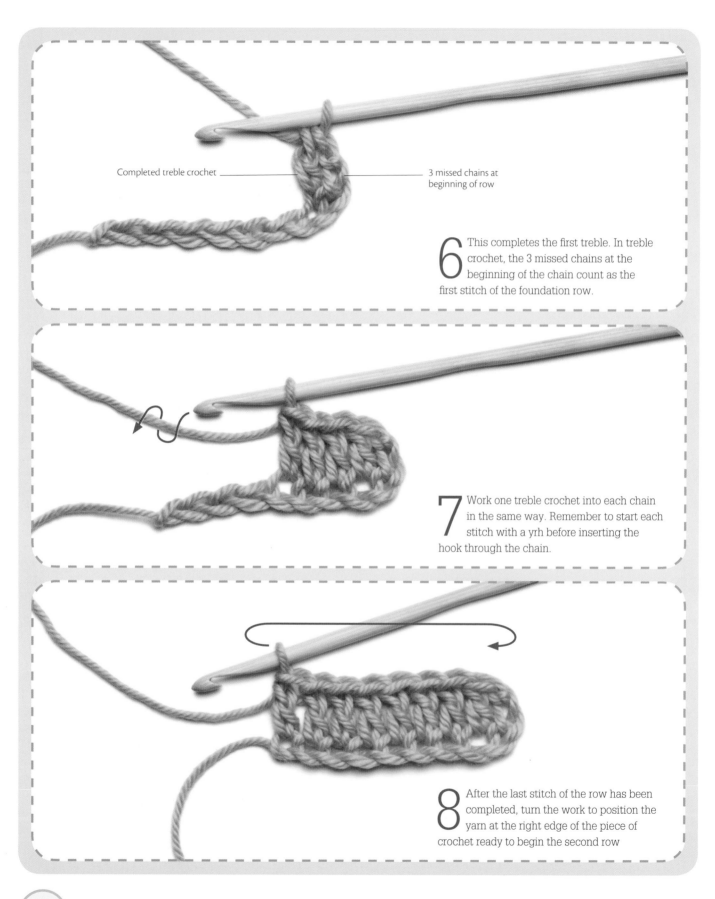

Completed treble crochet _____ 3 missed chains at
beginning of row

6 This completes the first treble. In treble
crochet, the 3 missed chains at the
beginning of the chain count as the
first stitch of the foundation row.

7 Work one treble crochet into each chain
in the same way. Remember to start each
stitch with a yrh before inserting the
hook through the chain.

8 After the last stitch of the row has been
completed, turn the work to position the
yarn at the right edge of the piece of
crochet ready to begin the second row

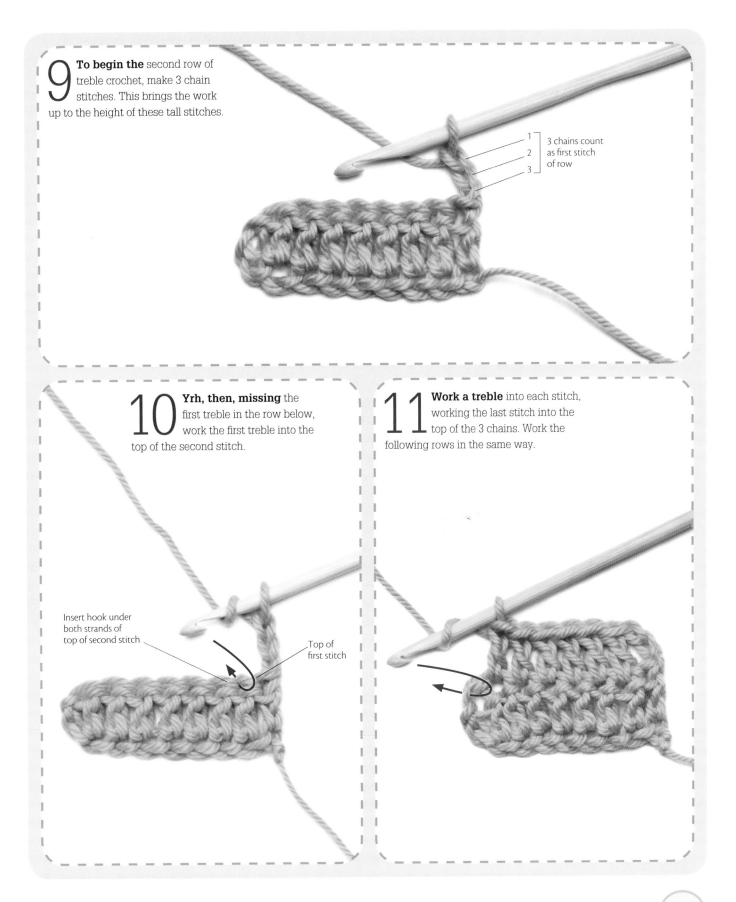

9 **To begin the** second row of treble crochet, make 3 chain stitches. This brings the work up to the height of these tall stitches.

1
2
3

3 chains count as first stitch of row

10 **Yrh, then, missing** the first treble in the row below, work the first treble into the top of the second stitch.

Insert hook under both strands of top of second stitch

Top of first stitch

11 **Work a treble** into each stitch, working the last stitch into the top of the 3 chains. Work the following rows in the same way.

A pretty bow transforms this simple headband into a child's hair accessory. The bow measures approximately 12cm x 5cm (5in x 2in).

The bow that is a striking feature in the child's version, above, is an optional extra. The headband looks just as good with or without it.

Pretty headband

A simple yet attractive band, this project makes use of treble crochet to create a strip that is then stitched together to make the headband. The child's size is given first, followed by an adult version in the variation box, below.

essential info ...

SIZE
46cm x 5cm (18in x 2in)

YARN
A: Child: Artesano DK 50g x 1

A

CROCHET HOOK
4mm hook

NOTIONS
Yarn needle

TENSION
17 tr per 10cm (4in)

Headband
Work 11 ch.

BAND
Row 1: 1 tr in 4th ch from hook and into each ch to end. Turn. (8sts)

Row 2: 3 ch, 1 tr in each tr to end of row. Turn.

Rep last row until work measures 46cm (18in) long or until desired length. Fasten off yarn.

Join strip at short ends to form a ring.

TIE
Cont in same yarn, work 11 ch.
Row 1: 1 tr in 4th ch from hook and into each ch to end. Turn. (8sts)

Row 2: 3 ch, 1 tr in each tr to end of row. Turn.

Rep last row 5 times more. (7 rows) Fasten off yarn.

Wrap short strip around the band at the seam to hide the seam. Sew the tie together at short ends to form a ring around the band.

BOW
Cont in same yarn, work 24 ch.
Row 1: 1 tr in 4th ch from hook and into each ch to end. Turn. (21sts)

Row 2: 3 ch, 1 tr in each tr to end of row. Turn.

Rep last row 3 further times. (5 rows)

Finishing
Fasten off yarn, weave in all ends. Slip the bow under the tie and secure with a couple of holding stitches.

variation ...

To make an adult-sized headband, make a chain of 14sts using Artesano DK in Fern (C743). Work Row 1, leaving you with 11sts and then repeat Row 2 until work measures 54cm (21¼ in). If you want to make a bow, too, work 28 ch and work as for the rest of the pattern, repeating Row 2 over 25sts 5 further times.

1 Whichever size you are making, to attach the tie, wrap it around the join of the headband, then sew the two short ends together.

2 Weave in loose ends and ensure that the seam is positioned at the back of the band so that it does not show.

Baby's cardigan

A beautiful cardigan for a very special baby, this project is sure to keep your favourite little one warm and cosy. The clever, simple construction incorporates the sleeves into the body of the cardigan so no seaming is needed, making this a particularly great introductory garment project.

essential info ...

SIZE
To fit a baby aged 0–6 (6–12) months

YARN
A: Jarol Heritage DK 100g x 2
B: Jarol Heritage DK 100g x 1

A   **B**

CROCHET HOOK
4mm hook

NOTIONS
3 buttons, approx 1cm (½in)
    in diameter
Yarn needle

TENSION
17 htr per 10cm (4in)

Cardigan

FRONT (Make 2)
Using yarn B, work 22 (25) ch.

Row 1: 1 htr into 3rd ch from hook, 1 htr into each ch to end. Turn. 20 (23)sts.

Row 2: 2 ch, 1 htr into each st across row. Turn. Change to yarn A and work straight in htr until piece measures 15 (16)cm/ 6 (6½)in.

Next row: 27(32) ch, 1 htr into 3rd ch from hook, then one htr into each ch to end of ch. 25 (30)sts increased for arm. Work across body stitches. 45 (53) htr Work straight on these sts until piece measures approx 20 (21)cm/8 (8½) in from hem, ending at arm edge.

Next row: Work across in htr to last 6 (8)sts, 1 dc into next st, turn leaving rem sts unworked for neck opening.

Next row: Ss across 5sts, htr to end of row. Work straight until piece measures 24 (25)cm/9½ (10)in to shoulder. Fasten off yarn.

BACK
Using yarn B, work 43 (47) ch.

Row 1: 1 htr into 3rd ch from hook, then 1 htr into each ch to end. Turn. 41(45) htr

Row 2: 2 ch, work 1 htr into each st across row. Turn. Change to yarn A and work straight in htr until piece measures the same as front to one row below armhole. Fasten off yarn.

Using yarn A, work 25 (30) ch, then work across body stitches in htr, work 27 (32) ch.

Next row: Work 1 htr into 3rd ch from hook, then 1 htr into each ch to end of ch. 25 (30)sts increased for arm. Work in htr across body stitches, then 1 htr into each ch to end for opposite arm. 50 (60)sts in total increased for arms. 91 (105) htr

Work straight on these sts until piece measures same as front to one row below shoulder.

Next row: Work across 35 (40)sts. Fasten off yarn, leaving rem sts unworked.

Fasten yarn to opposite arm edge, work across 35 (40)sts, fasten off yarn, leaving rem 21 (25)sts unworked for neck.

Finishing
Block all pieces lightly to shape. Sew shoulder seams, then sew up each underarm and side seam.

NECK EDGE
Rejoin yarn A to bottom of right front edge and work evenly in dc up edge, then round neck. At top of left edge, work 5 ch for button loop, then work 4 dc down edge, 5 ch, 4 dc, 5 ch, dc to bottom of left front. Sew buttons to right front, corresponding to the button loops.

CUFFS
Using yarn B, rejoin yarn to cuff and work 2 rows of dc evenly round. Weave in all ends.

The sleeves are made as part of the back and front pieces of the cardigan.

Rows of double crochet in a contrasting colour add a neat finishing touch to the cuffs and cardigan hem.

Double treble crochet

Worked in a very similar way to treble crochet, double treble crochet stitches are approximately one chain length taller because the stitch is begun with two wraps instead of one. Double trebles are often used in edging (see pp.86–89) and in medallions and flowers (see pp.120–125).

Working double treble stitch (abbreviation = dtr)

Identical on the front and the back, double treble crochet worked in rows is even softer than treble crochet. It also grows more quickly because the stitches are taller but not that much slower to work.

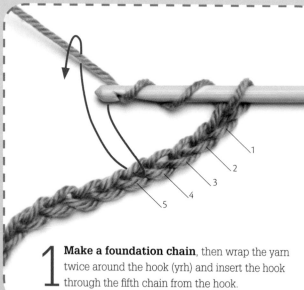

1 **Make a foundation chain**, then wrap the yarn twice around the hook (yrh) and insert the hook through the fifth chain from the hook.

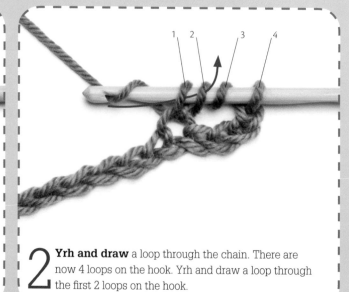

2 **Yrh and draw** a loop through the chain. There are now 4 loops on the hook. Yrh and draw a loop through the first 2 loops on the hook.

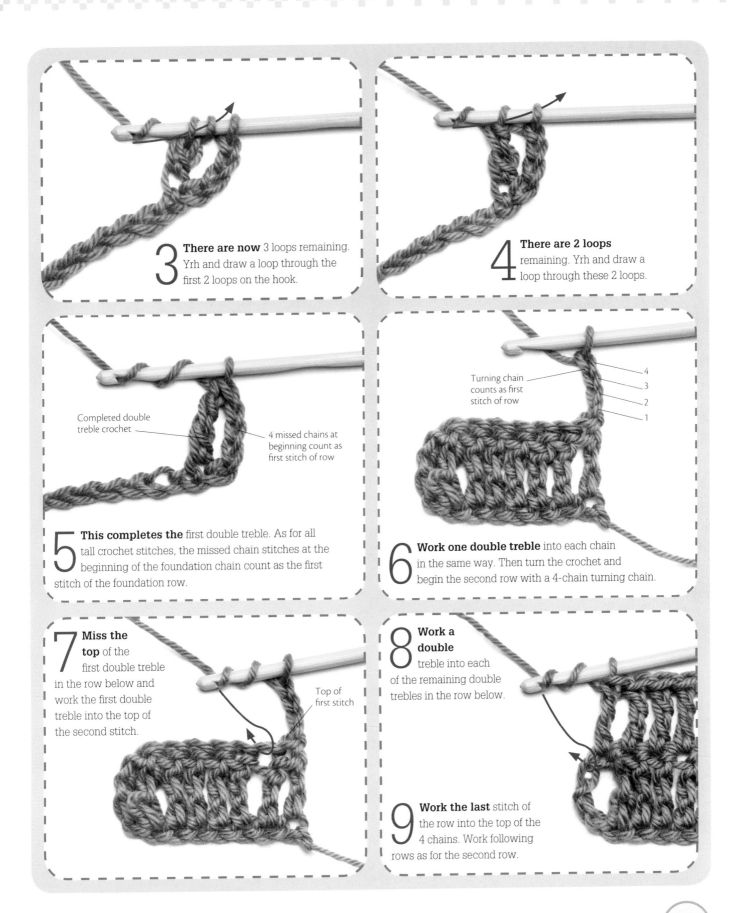

3 There are now 3 loops remaining. Yrh and draw a loop through the first 2 loops on the hook.

4 There are 2 loops remaining. Yrh and draw a loop through these 2 loops.

Completed double treble crochet

4 missed chains at beginning count as first stitch of row

5 This completes the first double treble. As for all tall crochet stitches, the missed chain stitches at the beginning of the foundation chain count as the first stitch of the foundation row.

Turning chain counts as first stitch of row

4
3
2
1

6 Work one double treble into each chain in the same way. Then turn the crochet and begin the second row with a 4-chain turning chain.

7 Miss the top of the first double treble in the row below and work the first double treble into the top of the second stitch.

Top of first stitch

8 Work a double treble into each of the remaining double trebles in the row below.

9 Work the last stitch of the row into the top of the 4 chains. Work following rows as for the second row.

Triple treble crochet

Stitches taller than double trebles are all worked in the same way as double trebles, except that more wraps are wound around the hook before the stitch is begun and they require taller turning chains. Once you can work triple trebles easily, you will be able to work quadruple and quintuple trebles without much effort.

Working triple treble stitch (abbreviation = trtr)

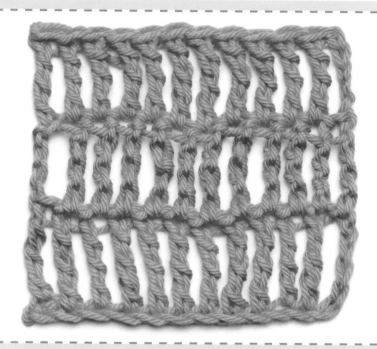

Triple treble crochet worked in rows looks the same on both sides of the fabric. Notice how airy the crochet texture becomes as the basic stitches get taller.

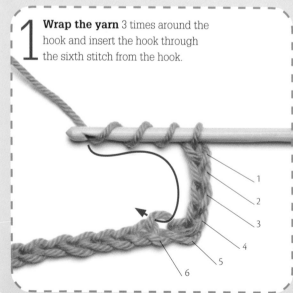

1 **Wrap the yarn** 3 times around the hook and insert the hook through the sixth stitch from the hook.

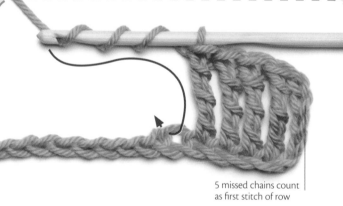

5 missed chains count as first stitch of row

2 **Work the loops** off the hook two at a time as for double trebles. Remember to wrap the yarn three times around the hook before starting each stitch. Start following rows with 5 chains.

Simple textures

The simplest and most subtle crochet textures are created by working into various parts of the stitches or between the stitches in the row below. Before trying out any of these techniques, learn about the parts of the stitches so you can identify them easily.

Parts of stitches

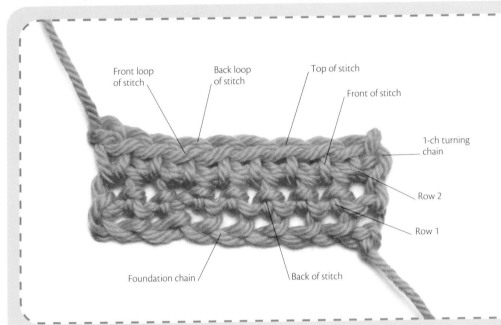

Front loop of stitch

Back loop of stitch

Top of stitch

Front of stitch

1-ch turning chain

Row 2

Row 1

Foundation chain

Back of stitch

Double crochet stitches: Work two rows of double crochet (see pp.40–42) and fasten off. Look closely at your sample and make sure you can identify all the parts of the stitch labelled on the left. If your crochet pattern tells you to work into the stitch below, always insert the hook under BOTH loops (the front loop and the back loop) at the top of the stitch as explained on p.42 for double crochet, unless it tells you to do otherwise.

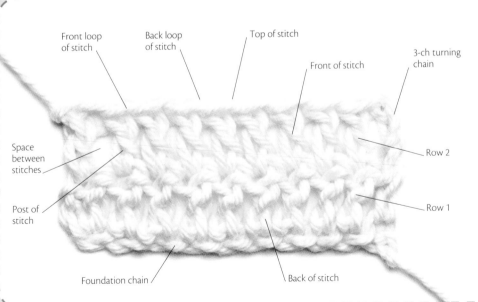

Front loop of stitch

Back loop of stitch

Top of stitch

Front of stitch

3-ch turning chain

Space between stitches

Post of stitch

Row 2

Row 1

Foundation chain

Back of stitch

Treble crochet stitches: Work two rows of treble crochet (see pp.46–49) and fasten off. Again, make sure you can identify all the parts of the stitch labelled on the left. As for double crochet and all other crochet stitches, if your crochet pattern tells you to work into the stitch below, always insert the hook under both loops at the top of the stitch, unless it tells you to do otherwise.

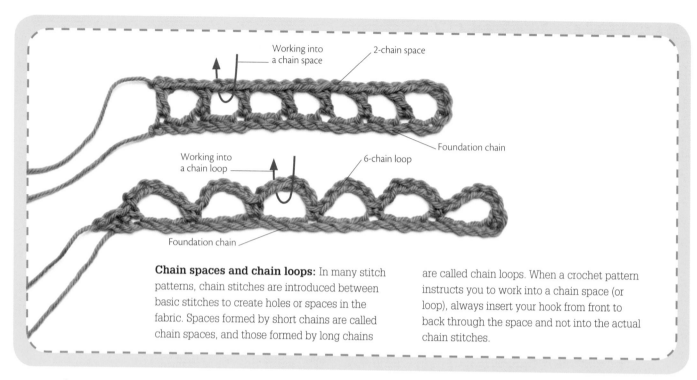

Working into a chain space

2-chain space

Working into a chain space

Foundation chain

Working into a chain loop

6-chain loop

Foundation chain

Chain spaces and chain loops: In many stitch patterns, chain stitches are introduced between basic stitches to create holes or spaces in the fabric. Spaces formed by short chains are called chain spaces, and those formed by long chains are called chain loops. When a crochet pattern instructs you to work into a chain space (or loop), always insert your hook from front to back through the space and not into the actual chain stitches.

Working into loops and spaces

Working into the back loop of a double crochet: Working into only the back loops of the stitches in every row of double crochet creates a deep ridged effect. The ridges are formed by the unworked loops.

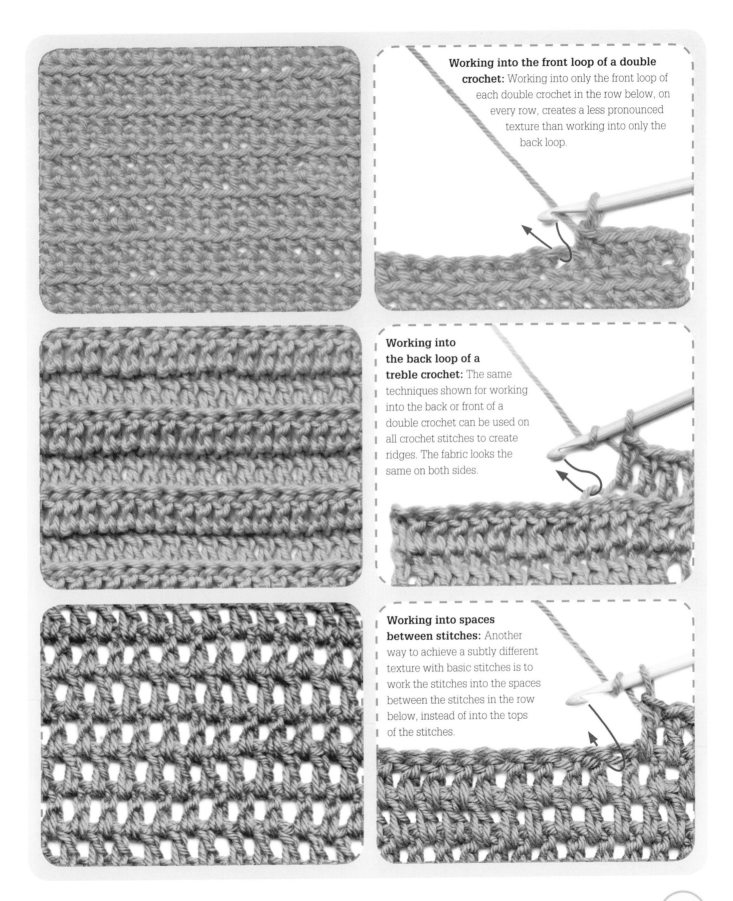

Working into the front loop of a double crochet: Working into only the front loop of each double crochet in the row below, on every row, creates a less pronounced texture than working into only the back loop.

Working into the back loop of a treble crochet: The same techniques shown for working into the back or front of a double crochet can be used on all crochet stitches to create ridges. The fabric looks the same on both sides.

Working into spaces between stitches: Another way to achieve a subtly different texture with basic stitches is to work the stitches into the spaces between the stitches in the row below, instead of into the tops of the stitches.

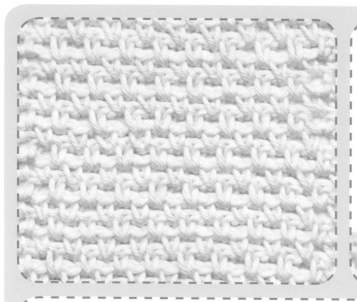

Working into a chain space: Tweed stitch illustrates the simplest of all textures created by working into a chain space. Here double crochet stitches are worked in the 1-chain spaces between the stitches in the row below, instead of into the tops of the stitches.

Tweed stitch pattern

Because it is such a popular stitch and a perfect alternative for basic double crochet, the pattern for it is given here. (See p.35 for abbreviations.) Start with an even number of chains.

Row 1: dc in 2nd ch from hook, *1 ch, miss next ch, 1 dc in next ch; rep from * to end. Turn.

Row 2: 1 ch (does NOT count as a stitch), 1 dc in first dc, 1 dc in next 1-ch sp, *1 ch, 1 dc in next 1-ch sp; rep from * to last dc, 1 dc in last dc. Turn.

Row 3: 1 ch (does NOT count as a stitch), 1 dc in first dc, *1 ch, 1 dc in next 1-ch sp; rep from * to last 2 dc, 1 ch, miss next dc, 1 dc in last dc. Turn.

Rep rows 2 and 3 to form patt.

Front post treble

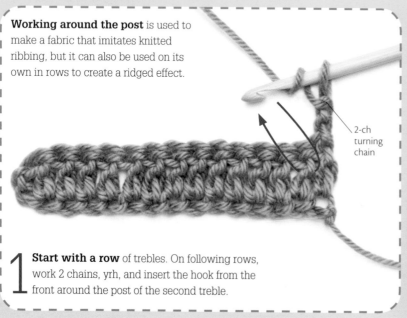

Working around the post is used to make a fabric that imitates knitted ribbing, but it can also be used on its own in rows to create a ridged effect.

2-ch turning chain

1 **Start with a row** of trebles. On following rows, work 2 chains, yrh, and insert the hook from the front around the post of the second treble.

2 **To complete the** treble, yrh and draw a loop through, then [yrh and draw through the first 2 loops on the hook] twice as shown by the two large arrows.

3 **Work a treble** around each of the following trebles in the row below in the same way.

4 **At the end** of the row, work a treble into the top of the turning chain. Repeat the second row to form a ridged texture.

Back post treble

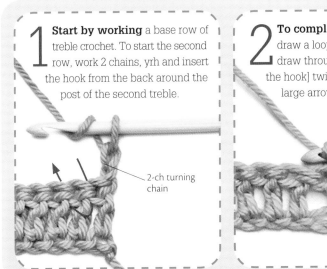

1 **Start by working** a base row of treble crochet. To start the second row, work 2 chains, yrh and insert the hook from the back around the post of the second treble.

2-ch turning chain

2 **To complete the** treble, yrh and draw a loop through, then [yrh and draw through the first 2 loops on the hook] twice as shown by the two large arrows.

3 **Work a treble** around each of the trebles in the row below in the same way. Continue as for step 4 of Front post treble (opposite).

Shells

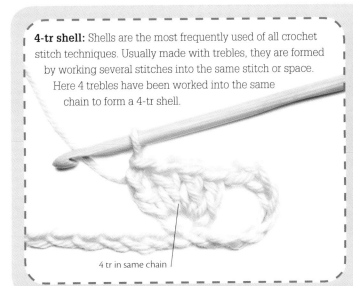

4-tr shell: Shells are the most frequently used of all crochet stitch techniques. Usually made with trebles, they are formed by working several stitches into the same stitch or space. Here 4 trebles have been worked into the same chain to form a 4-tr shell.

4 tr in same chain

5-tr shell: Here 5 trebles have been worked into the same chain to form a 5-tr shell. Any number of trebles can be used to form a shell, but the most commonly used crochet shells have 2, 3, 4, 5, or 6 stitches. Shells can also be made with half trebles and taller basic stitches.

5 tr in same chain

Cold-weather scarf

Suitably masculine, this warm scarf has a chunky textured appearance. It is made by working back and forth in rows using a crochet rib stitch and is a great introduction to the technique of crocheting around the post of a stitch. For more information on front post and back post trebles, see pp.60–61.

essential info ...

SIZE
18cm x 130cm (7in x 51in) or
    desired length

YARN
A: Rowan Colourspun 50g x 4

A

CROCHET HOOK
5mm hook

NOTIONS
Yarn needle

Special notes

fptr: front post treble. Yrh and insert hook around the post of next st, taking hook from front to back to front, yrh and pull up a loop, yrh and pull through two loops, yrh and pull through last two loops.

bptr: back post treble. Yrh and insert hook around the post of next st, taking hook from back to front to back, yrh and pull up a loop, yrh and pull through two loops, yrh and pull through last two loops.

Scarf

Work 34 ch.

Row 1: 1 tr in 4th ch from hook, 1 tr in each ch to end, turn.

Row 2: 2 ch, miss first tr, fptr around next st, bptr around next st; rep from * to end, tr in top of turning ch at end, turn.

Rep row 2 until piece measures 130cm (51in), or desired length (additional balls of yarn will be required to make scarf longer).

Fasten off, weave in all ends.

The crochet rib stitch forms deep, textured ridges that help trap heat, making the scarf warm and cosy

The gently variagated yarn used for this project forms subtle stripes when worked back and forth in rows.

Rows of deep rib stitch create a scarf so wonderfully warm and thick it will keep the wearer toasty in even the coldest weather. The variegated yarn adds interest to an otherwise simple pattern.

Clutch bag

This elegant clutch is crocheted in a softly shimmering mercerized cotton and is just big enough to hold all your essentials for an evening out. It is made in rows using a cluster and shell stitch and forms its own edging and buttonholes. This is a quick and easy project – why not crochet one for tonight?

essential info ...

SIZE
20cm x 10cm (8in x 4in)

YARN
A: Rico Essentials Cotton DK 50g x 1

A

CROCHET HOOK
3.5mm hook

NOTIONS
1 x 2cm (¾) shell button
Yarn needle

Special notes

Cluster: over next 5sts, (which include 2 tr, 1 dc, 2 tr), work [yrh and insert hook in next st, yrh and draw a loop through, yrh and draw through first two loops on hook] 5 times (6 loops on hook), yrh and draw through all 6 loops on hook.

Pattern

Work 46 ch.

Row 1: 2 tr in 4th ch from hook, miss next 2 chs, 1 dc in next ch, *miss next 2 chs, 5 tr in next ch, miss next 2 chs, 1 dc in next ch; rep from * to last 3 chs, miss next 2 chs, 3 tr in last ch, turn.

Row 2: 1 ch, 1 dc in first tr, *2 ch, 1 cluster over next 5sts, 2 ch, 1 dc in centre tr of 5-tr group; rep from * to end, working last dc of last rep in top of 3-ch at end, turn.

Row 3: 3 ch, 2 tr in first dc, miss next 2 chs, 1 dc in next st (top of first cluster), miss next 2 chs, *5 tr in next dc, miss next 2 chs, 1 dc in next st (top of next cluster); rep from *, ending with 3 tr in last dc, turn.

Rep rows 2 and 3 until piece measures 25cm (10in), ending on a row 3.

Fasten off, weave in all ends.

Finishing

Fold at 10cm (4in) and sew (or use slip stitch seam, see p.135) 2 sides to form pocket. Fold top flap over and attach button.

tips ...

You may choose to line your clutch with fabric, or place a piece of card inside to help it keep its shape.

The cluster and shell stitch pattern forms its own decorative edge so there is no need to add edging.

Simple lace techniques

A few openwork stitch patterns are explained here to provide an introduction to some popular openwork crochet techniques – chain loops, shells, and picots.

Chain loop mesh

1 **After working the first row** of chain loops into the foundation chain as explained to the right, work the 5-chain loops of the following rows into the loops below, joining them on with a dc as shown here.

2 **Remember to work** the last dc of each row into the space inside the turning chain made at the beginning of the previous row. If you don't, your lace will become narrower.

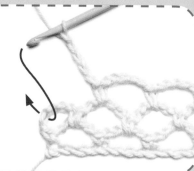

crochet instructions

Make a multiple of 4 ch, plus 2 extra.

Row 1: 1 dc in 6th ch from hook, *5 ch, miss next 3 ch, 1 dc in next ch; rep from * to end, turn.

Row 2: *5 ch, 1 dc in next 5-ch loop; rep from * to end, turn.

Rep row 2 to form patt.

Shell mesh stitch

1 **On the shell row** of this stitch (see opposite, top), start each shell with a dc in a chain loop. Then work all the tr of the shell into a single dc as shown.

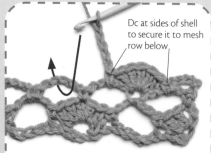

Dc at sides of shell to secure it to mesh row below

2 **Complete the shell** with a dc worked into the following chain loop. Then work a chain loop and join it to the next chain loop with a dc as shown.

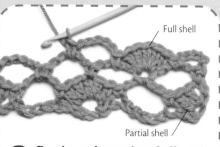

Full shell

Partial shell

3 **Continue alternating shells** and chain loops to complete the shell row.

4 **Work mesh and shell rows** alternately, working partial shells at ends on alternate shell rows.

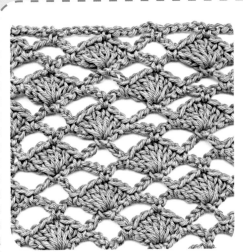

crochet instructions

Make a multiple of 12 ch, plus 4 extra.

Row 1 (RS): 2 tr in 4th ch from hook, *miss next 2 ch, 1 dc in next ch, 5 ch, miss next 5 ch, 1 dc in next ch, miss next 2 ch, 5 tr in next ch; rep from *, ending last rep with 3 tr (instead of 5 tr) in last ch, turn.

Row 2: 1 ch (does NOT count as a st), 1 dc in first tr, *5 ch, 1 dc in next 5-ch loop, 5 ch, 1 dc in 3rd tr of next 5-tr shell; rep from * working last dc of last rep in top of 3-ch at end, turn.

Row 3: *5 ch, 1 dc in next 5-ch loop, 5 tr in next dc, 1 dc in next 5-ch loop; rep from *, ending with 2 ch, 1 tr in last dc, turn.

Row 4: 1 ch (does NOT count as a st), 1 dc in first tr, *5 ch, 1 dc in 3rd tr of next 5-tr shell, 5 ch, 1 dc in next 5-ch loop; rep from * to end, turn.

Row 5: 3 ch (counts as first tr), 2 tr in first dc, *1 dc in next 5-ch loop, 5 ch, 1 dc in next 5-ch loop, 5 tr in next dc; rep from * ending last rep with 3 tr (instead of 5 tr) in last dc, turn.

Rep rows 2–5 to form patt.

Picot net stitch

1 **In this stitch pattern** (see right), work 4 chains for each picot. Close the picot-ring by working a slip stitch in the fourth chain from the hook as shown.

2 **Work 3 dc** between each of the picots in each picot row as shown.

3 **After each picot row,** work a 2-chain space above each picot and a tr between the picots as shown.

crochet instructions

Make a multiple of 3 ch, plus 2 extra.

Row 1 (RS): 1 dc in 2nd ch from hook, 1 dc in next ch, *4 ch, 1 ss in 4th ch from hook (called 1 picot), 1 dc in each of next 3 ch; rep from * omitting 1 dc at end of last rep, turn.

Row 2: 5 ch (counts as 1 tr and a 2-ch sp), miss first 3 dc (which includes 2 dc before picot and 1 dc after picot), 1 tr in next dc, *2 ch, miss next 2 dc (which includes 1 dc on each side of picot), 1 tr in next dc; rep from * to end, turn.

Row 3: 1 ch (does NOT count as a st), 1 dc in first tr, *work [1 dc, 1 picot, 1 dc] all in next 2-ch sp, 1 dc in next tr; rep from * working last dc of last rep in 3rd ch from last tr, turn.

Rep rows 2 and 3 to form patt.

Fans stitch creates rows of asymmetrical spaces, bringing a sense of lightness to this gorgeous scarf. Because it's made in a wool blend, it's surprisingly warm, too.

Lacy scarf

This lacy, openwork scarf is made using fans stitch. The openwork pattern is created using alternating chain loops and treble crochet stitches. It is an easy first project as it's very forgiving!

essential info ...

SIZE
18cm x 180cm (7in x 71in) or desired length

YARN
A: Sirdar Country Style DK 100g x 1

A

CROCHET HOOK
4mm hook
Yarn needle

Scarf

Work 33 ch.

Row 1: 1 tr in 5th ch from hook, *2 ch, miss 5 chs, 3 tr in next ch, 2 ch, tr in next ch; rep from * 3 times more.

Row 2: 4 ch, turn. 1 tr in first 2-ch sp, *2 ch, work (4 tr, 2 ch, 1 tr) in next 2-ch sp; rep from * twice more, 2 ch, work 3 tr in last sp and 1 tr in 3rd of 4 chs of turning ch from row below.

Rep row 2 until piece is 180cm (71in) or desired length.

Fasten off, weave in all ends.

The alternating pattern forms rows of asymmetrical stitches and spaces, giving the scarf a light, lacy appearance.

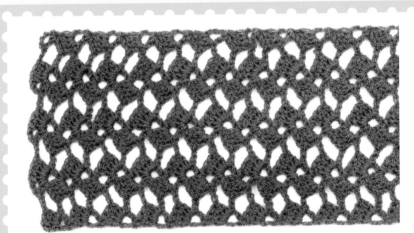

tips ...

There is no need to add edging to either the long sides or the ends of this scarf as the stitch pattern forms its own.

Simple stripes

Stripes worked in basic stitches have more potential for creativity than most crocheters realize. The only techniques you need to learn is how and when to change colours to start a new stripe, and how to carry the yarns up the side edge of the crochet.

Changing colours

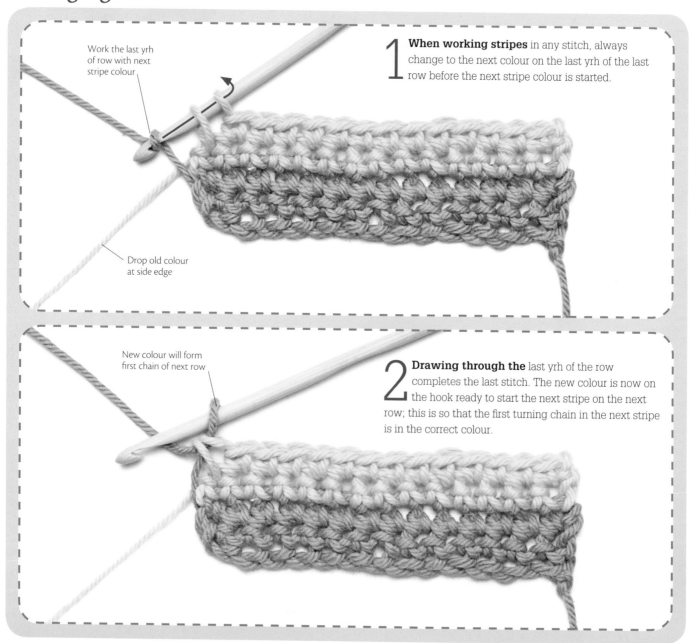

Work the last yrh of row with next stripe colour

Drop old colour at side edge

1 **When working stripes** in any stitch, always change to the next colour on the last yrh of the last row before the next stripe colour is started.

New colour will form first chain of next row

2 **Drawing through the** last yrh of the row completes the last stitch. The new colour is now on the hook ready to start the next stripe on the next row; this is so that the first turning chain in the next stripe is in the correct colour.

Carrying colours up side edge

If a colour is not needed for more than 2 rows, wrap it around the other colour to secure it. If it is not needed for more than 8 rows, cut it off and rejoin it later.

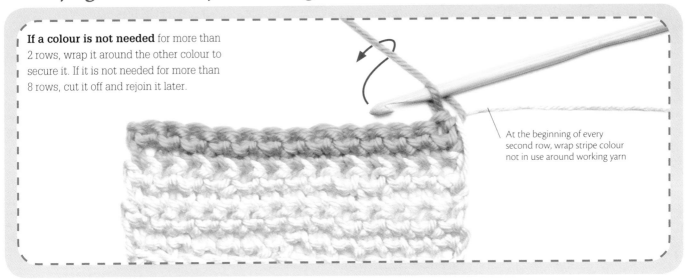

At the beginning of every second row, wrap stripe colour not in use around working yarn

Stripe combinations

Smooth wool and fuzzy mohair stripe: The repeated double crochet stripe sequence here is two rows of a smooth wool yarn and two rows of a fuzzy mohair yarn, so each colour can simply be dropped at the side of the work and picked up when it is needed again.

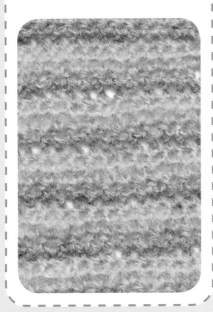

Three-colour stripe: This double crochet stripe has a repeated sequence of two rows of each of three colours. Wrap the working yarn around the colours not in use on every second row to keep them snug against the edge. When changing colours, pull in the new colour firmly but not too tightly or it will pucker the edge.

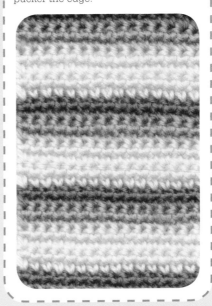

Double crochet and treble crochet stripe: Each of the two stripes in this design is two rows tall. One stripe is worked in double crochet and the other in treble crochet. Adding in the taller trebles gives the crochet fabric a softer texture.

Bag of stripes

Changing colours is a fun way to liven up a simple strip of double crochet. A length of crochet is useful for lots of projects; here it's a handy bag.

essential info ...

SIZE
13cm x 10cm (5in x 4in)

YARN
Cotton yarn in various colours

CROCHET HOOK
4.5mm hook

NOTIONS
1 x 2.5cm (1in) button
Yarn needle

Bag

Work 16 ch.

Row 1: Make 3 ch, tr into 4th ch from hook, 1 tr into each ch to end. Turn. (16sts)

Row 2: Make 1 ch, dc into each ch to end. Turn.

Cont working rows in dc, changing colours to create stripes (see pp.70–71). In this design the stripes are 3 to 4 rows deep, but the number of stripes is up to you. The length of stripes in this crochet measures about 23cm (9in).

Next row: Make 3 ch, tr into 4th ch from hook, 1 tr into each ch to end. Turn.

Cont working rows in dc until the length of crochet measures 30cm (12in).

Fasten off, weave in all ends.

Finishing

Neaten the loose ends (see below). Fold the work over, leaving room at the top for the flap. Stitch the two edges together using overstitch, then sew up both sides and turn the work inside out. Make a button loop. Push the hook through the crochet, loop the yarn over the hook and pull the hook back through the crochet. Tie together the loose ends of the yarn and sew on the button.

For the button loop, cut a piece of yarn 10cm (4in) long. Place the ends through the loop and tie a knot to create a loop for the button.

tips...

Tidy up the loose ends by threading the ends onto a darning needle and sewing them along the edge of the work.

This size of bag is perfect for storing all your crochet bits and bobs. Make a bigger one for larger pieces of equipment.

Simple colourwork stitch patterns

Crochet colourwork stitch patterns are great fun to work. This selection of stitches, all easy to work, includes an array of textures, so you are sure to find one that catches your eye. Although some of the stitches have a right and wrong side, the back and front of these fabrics still look very similar. The reversibility of crochet is one of its best features. If you want to make a scarf, shawl, baby blanket, throw, or cushion cover with one of these stitches, take your time to choose the right colour combination (see below). See pp.34–35 for a list of the abbreviations that are used here.

Simple zigzag stitch

crochet instructions

This pattern is worked in 3 colours (A, B, C).
Using C, make a multiple of 16 ch, plus 2 extra.

Row 1: (RS) Using A, 2 dc in 2nd ch from hook, *1 dc in each of next 7 ch, miss next ch, 1 dc in each of next 7 ch, 3 dc in next ch; rep from * to end, working 2 dc (instead of 3 dc) in last ch, turn.

Row 2: Using A, 1 ch (does NOT count as a st), 2 dc in first dc, *1 dc in each of next 7 dc, miss next 2 dc, 1 dc in each of next 7 dc, 3 dc in next dc; rep from * to end, working 2 dc (instead of 3 dc) in last dc, turn.

Rows 3 and 4: Using B, rep row 2.

Rows 5 and 6: Using C, [rep row 2] twice.

Rows 7 and 8: Using A, [rep row 2] twice.

Rep rows 3–8 to form patt.

Choosing yarn colours

Choose yarn colours with care. Always buy only one ball of each colour first and test that the colours work well together. For a successful combination, the chosen colours should stand out well against each other, either in tone (darkness and lightness) or in hue. It is best to work several colour combinations before deciding on the final one, especially if the item you are making is a large one like a blanket. Pin the swatches up and stand back to study them – the right one will pop right out at you.

Triangles spike stitch

crochet instructions

NOTE: spike st = do not work into next st, but instead insert hook front to back through top of st 1, 2, or 3 rows below this st, yrh and draw a loop through, lengthening the loop to the height of the row being worked (and enclosing the missed st), yrh and draw through both loops on hook to complete an elongated dc.

This pattern is worked in 2 colours (A, B).
Using A, make a multiple of 4 ch.

Row 1: (RS) Using A, 1 dc in 2nd ch from hook, 1 dc in each of rem ch, turn.

Row 2: Using A, 1 ch (does NOT count as a st), 1 dc in each dc to end, turn.

Rows 3 and 4: Using A, [rep row 2] twice.

Row 5: (RS) Using B, 1 ch (does NOT count as a st), 1 dc in first dc, *1 dc in next dc, 1 spike st in top of dc one row below next dc, 1 spike st in top of dc 2 rows below next dc, 1 spike st in top of dc 3 rows below next dc; rep from * to last 2 dc, 1 dc in each of last 2 dc, turn.

Rows 6, 7, and 8: Using B, [rep row 2] 3 times.

Row 9: (RS) Using A, rep row 5.

Rep rows 2–9: to form patt, ending with a patt row 5 or 9.

Gem stitch

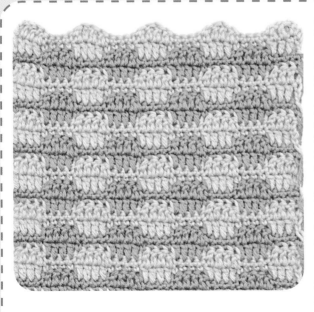

crochet instructions

This pattern is worked in 2 colours (A, B).
Using A, make a multiple of 8 ch, plus 5 extra.

Row 1: (RS) Using A, 1 dc in 2nd ch from hook, 1 dc in each of next 3 ch, *1 tr in each of next 4 ch, 1 dc in each of next 4 ch; rep from * to end, turn.

Row 2: Using A, 1 ch (does NOT count as a st), 1 dc in each of first 4 dc, *1 tr in each of next 4 tr, 1 dc in each of next 4 dc; rep from * to end, turn.

Row 3: Using B, 3 ch (counts as first tr), miss first dc, 1 tr in each of next 3 dc, *1 dc in each of next 4 tr, 1 tr in each of next 4 dc; rep from * to end, turn.

Row 4: Using B, 3 ch (counts as first tr), miss first tr, 1 tr in each of next 3 tr, *1 dc in each of next 4 dc, 1 tr in each of next 4 tr; rep from * to end, working last tr of last rep in top of 3-ch at end, turn.

Row 5: Using A, 1 ch (does NOT count as a st), 1 dc in each of first 4 tr, *1 tr in each of next 4 dc, 1 dc in each of next 4 tr; rep from * working last dc of last rep in top of 3-ch at end, turn.

Rep rows 2–5 to form patt.

Double zigzag stitch

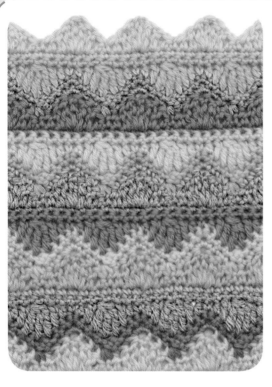

Crochet instructions

NOTE: cluster (also called dtr3tog) = [yrh twice and insert hook in next st, yrh and draw a loop through, (yrh and draw through first 2 loops on hook) twice] 3 times (4 loops now on hook), yrh and draw through all 4 loops on hook; dtr2tog = [yrh twice and insert hook in next st, yrh and draw a loop through, (yrh and draw through first 2 loops on hook) twice] twice (3 loops now on hook), yrh and draw through all 3 loops on hook.

This pattern is worked in 4 colours (A, B, C, D).
Make a multiple of 6 ch, plus 2 extra. Work the following rows in stripes, repeating this stripe sequence – 2 rows A, 2 rows B, 2 rows C, 2 rows D.

Row 1: (RS) 1 dc in 2nd ch from hook, 1 dc in each of rem ch, turn.

Row 2: 1 ch (does NOT count as a st), 1 dc in first dc, *1 htr in next dc, 1 tr in next dc, 3 dtr in next dc, 1 tr in next dc, 1 htr in next dc, 1 dc in next dc; rep from * to end, turn.

Row 3: 1 ch (does NOT count as a st), dc2tog over first 2sts, 1 dc in each of next 2sts, *3 dc in next st, 1 dc in each of next 2sts, dc3tog over next 3sts, 1 dc in each of next 2sts; rep from * to last 5sts, 3 dc in next st, 1 dc in each of next 2sts, dc2tog over last 2sts, turn.

Row 4: Rep row 3.

Row 5: 4 ch, miss first st, 1 dtr in next dc (counts as first dtr2tog), 1 tr in next dc, 1 htr in next dc, 1 dc in next dc, 1 htr in next dc, 1 tr in next dc, *1 cluster over next 3sts, 1 tr in next dc, 1 htr in next dc, 1 dc in next dc, 1 htr in next dc, 1 tr in next dc; rep from *, ending with dtr2tog over last 2sts, turn.

Row 6: 1 ch (does NOT count as a st), 1 dc in first st, 1 dc in next st and each st to end (do NOT work a dc in top of 4-ch turning ch at end), turn.

Row 7: 1 ch (does NOT count as a st), 1 dc in each dc to end, turn.
Rep rows 2–7 to form patt, while continuing stripe sequence.

Coloured tweed stitch

crochet instructions

This pattern is worked in 3 colours (A, B, C).
Using A, make a multiple of 2 ch.

Row 1: Using A, 1 dc in 2nd ch from hook, *1 ch, miss next ch, 1 dc in next ch; rep from * to end, turn.

Row 2: Using B, 1 ch (does NOT count as a st), 1 dc in first dc, 1 dc in next 1-ch sp, *1 ch, 1 dc in next 1-ch sp; rep from * to last dc, 1 dc in last dc, turn.

Row 3: Using C, 1 ch (does NOT count as a st), 1 dc in first dc, *1 ch, 1 dc in next 1-ch sp; rep from * to last 2 dc, 1 ch, miss next dc, 1 dc in last dc, turn.

Row 4: Using A, rep row 2.

Row 5: Using B, rep row 3.

Row 6: Using C, rep row 2.

Row 7: Using A, rep row 3.

Rep rows 2–7 to form patt.

Bobble stripe

crochet instructions

NOTE: bobble = [yrh and insert hook in specified st, yrh and draw a loop through, yrh and draw through first 2 loops on hook] 3 times all in same st (4 loops now on hook), yrh and draw through all 4 loops on hook to complete 3-tr bobble.

This pattern is worked in 3 colours (A, B, C).
Using A, make a multiple of 2 ch, plus 1 extra.
Work the following rows in stripes, repeating this stripe sequence – 1 row A, 1 row B, 1 row C.

Row 1: (WS) 1 htr in 3rd ch from hook, *miss next ch, work [1 htr, 1 ch, 1 htr] all in next ch; rep from * to last 2 ch, miss next ch, 2 htr in last ch, turn.

Row 2: (RS) 3 ch (counts as first tr), 1 tr in first htr, *1 ch, 1 bobble in next 1-ch sp; rep from *, ending with 1 ch, work [yrh and insert hook in top of 2-ch at end of row, yrh and draw a loop through, yrh and draw through first 2 loops on hook] twice all in same place (3 loops now on hook), yrh and draw through all 3 loops on hook, turn.

Row 3: 2 ch (counts as first htr), *work [1 htr, 1 ch, 1 htr] all in next 1-ch sp; rep from *, ending with 1 htr in top of 3-ch, turn.

Row 4: 3 ch (counts as first tr), 1 bobble in next 1-ch sp, *1 ch, 1 bobble in next 1-ch sp; rep from *, ending with 1 tr in top of 2-ch at end, turn.

Row 5: 2 ch (counts as first htr), 1 htr in first tr, *work [1 htr, 1 ch, 1 htr] all in next 1-ch sp; rep from *, ending with 2 htr in top of 3-ch at end, turn.

Rep rows 2–5 to form patt, while continuing stripe sequence.

Spike stitch stripes

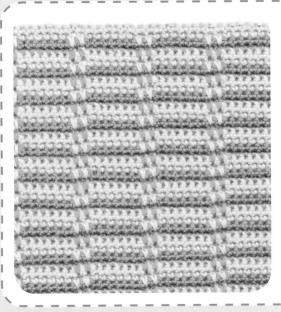

crochet instructions

NOTE: spike st = do not work into next st, but instead insert hook front to back through top of st one row below this st, yrh and draw a loop through, lengthening the loop to the height of the row being worked (and enclosing the missed st), yrh and draw through both loops on hook to complete an elongated dc.

This pattern is worked in 2 colours (A, B).
Using A, make a multiple of 8 ch, plus 1 extra.

Row 1: (RS) Using A, 1 dc in 2nd ch from hook, 1 dc in each of rem ch, turn.

Row 2: Using A, 1 ch (does NOT count as a st), 1 dc in each dc to end, turn.

Row 3: Using B, 1 ch (does NOT count as a st), *1 dc in each of next 3 dc, [1 spike st in top of st one row below next st] twice, 1 dc in each of next 3 dc; rep from * to end, turn.

Row 4: Using B, rep row 2.

Row 5: Using A, rep row 3.

Rep rows 2–5 to form patt.

Chevron cushion

A great introduction to colourwork, this project uses zigzag stitch (see p.74). The entire cushion cover is made in one piece and then stitched up the sides, as explained in the finishing section, below.

essential info ...

SIZE
40cm x 30cm (16in x 12in)

YARN
A: Sirdar Click DK 50g x 2
B: Sirdar Country Style DK 50g x 1

A   B

CROCHET HOOK
4mm hook

NOTIONS
Cushion pad 40cm x 30cm
(16in x 12in) (or size required
for your cushion cover)
5 x 1.5cm (½in) buttons
Yarn needle

Cushion

With yarn B, work 81 ch.

Row 1: 1 dc in 2nd ch from hook, 1 dc in each ch to end, turn. (80sts)

Rows 2–3: 1 ch, 2 dc in next st, 1 dc in each of next 7sts, miss next 2 dc, 1 dc in each of next 7sts, *2 dc in each of next 2sts, 1 dc in each of next 7sts, miss next 2 dc, 1 dc in each of next 7sts; rep from * to last st, 2 dc in last st. Turn.

Change to yarn A.
Rows 4–6: 2 ch, 2 htr in next st, 1 htr in each of next 7sts, miss next 2sts, 1 htr in each of next 7sts, *2 htr in each of next 2sts, 1 htr in each of next 7sts, miss next 2 dc, 1 htr in each of next 7sts; rep from * to last st, 2 htr in last st. Turn.

Change to yarn B.
Row 7: 1 ch, 2 dc in next st, 1 dc in each of next 7sts, miss next 2 dc, 1 dc in each of next 7sts, *2 dc in each of next 2sts, 1 dc in each of next 7sts, miss next 2 dc, 1 dc in each of next 7sts; rep from * to last st, 2 dc in last st. Turn.

Change to yarn A.
Rep last 4 rows until work measures approximately 70cm (28in), or desired length – long enough to fit comfortably around a cushion with an overlap.

End with a row 7, then rep row 7 twice more in yarn B.

Fasten off, weave in all ends.

Finishing

Block piece lightly to shape (see p.132). Wrap piece around cushion pad, with an overlap halfway down back of pad. Ensure top edge of piece, with 5 complete points, is on top, overlapping bottom of piece. Sew up bottom two side seams of cushion, then sew down top two side seams, overlapping bottom seam. Fasten middle flap of cushion by sewing buttons on bottom edge of piece, corresponding to first decrease hole in yarn A htr row next to end of each point. Fasten buttons and weave in all ends.

tips ...

The stitch pattern forms a neat zigzag edge to the cushion cover. The buttons are simply pushed through holes in the pattern.

The buttonholes are created
as part of the pattern.

Buttons are fixed to the
bottom layer of the cushion
cover at the bottom of each
"V" in the zigzag pattern.

Shaping crochet

To move from making simple squares and rectangles, a crocheter needs to know how to increase and decrease the number of stitches in the row to make shaped pieces. The most commonly used simple shaping techniques are provided here.

Double crochet increases

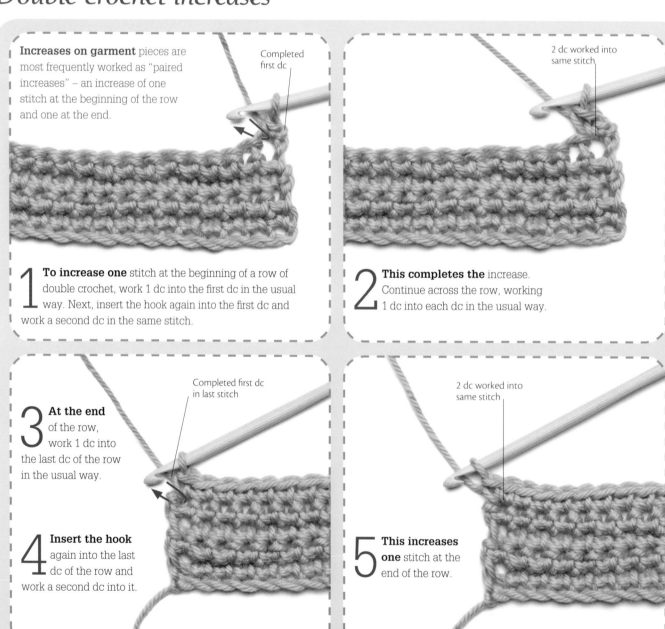

Increases on garment pieces are most frequently worked as "paired increases" – an increase of one stitch at the beginning of the row and one at the end.

Completed first dc

1 **To increase one** stitch at the beginning of a row of double crochet, work 1 dc into the first dc in the usual way. Next, insert the hook again into the first dc and work a second dc in the same stitch.

2 dc worked into same stitch

2 **This completes the** increase. Continue across the row, working 1 dc into each dc in the usual way.

Completed first dc in last stitch

3 **At the end** of the row, work 1 dc into the last dc of the row in the usual way.

4 **Insert the hook** again into the last dc of the row and work a second dc into it.

2 dc worked into same stitch

5 **This increases one** stitch at the end of the row.

Treble crochet increases

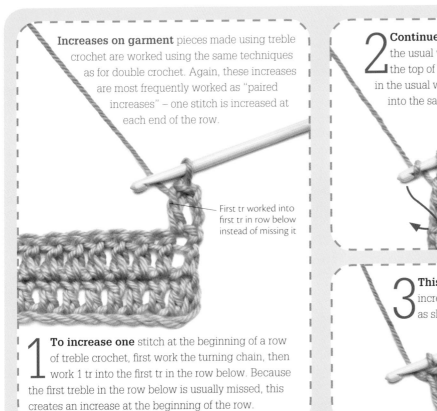

Increases on garment pieces made using treble crochet are worked using the same techniques as for double crochet. Again, these increases are most frequently worked as "paired increases" – one stitch is increased at each end of the row.

1 **To increase one** stitch at the beginning of a row of treble crochet, first work the turning chain, then work 1 tr into the first tr in the row below. Because the first treble in the row below is usually missed, this creates an increase at the beginning of the row.

First tr worked into first tr in row below instead of missing it

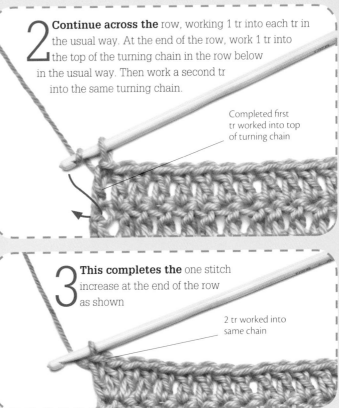

2 **Continue across the** row, working 1 tr into each tr in the usual way. At the end of the row, work 1 tr into the top of the turning chain in the row below in the usual way. Then work a second tr into the same turning chain.

Completed first tr worked into top of turning chain

3 **This completes the** one stitch increase at the end of the row as shown

2 tr worked into same chain

Step increase at beginning of row

1 **Increases are also** frequently worked in crochet so that they form little steps at the edge. As an example, to add a 3-stitch step increase at the beginning of a row of double crochet, begin by making 4 chains as shown here. (Always make one chain more than the number of extra double crochets required.)

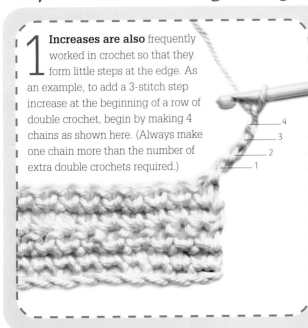

4
3
2
1

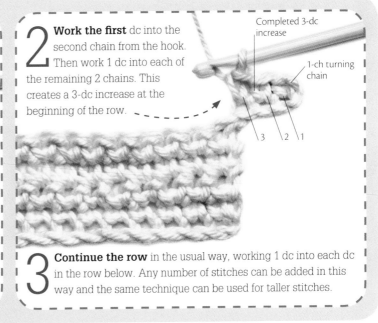

2 **Work the first** dc into the second chain from the hook. Then work 1 dc into each of the remaining 2 chains. This creates a 3-dc increase at the beginning of the row.

Completed 3-dc increase

1-ch turning chain

3 2 1

3 **Continue the row** in the usual way, working 1 dc into each dc in the row below. Any number of stitches can be added in this way and the same technique can be used for taller stitches.

Step increase at end of row

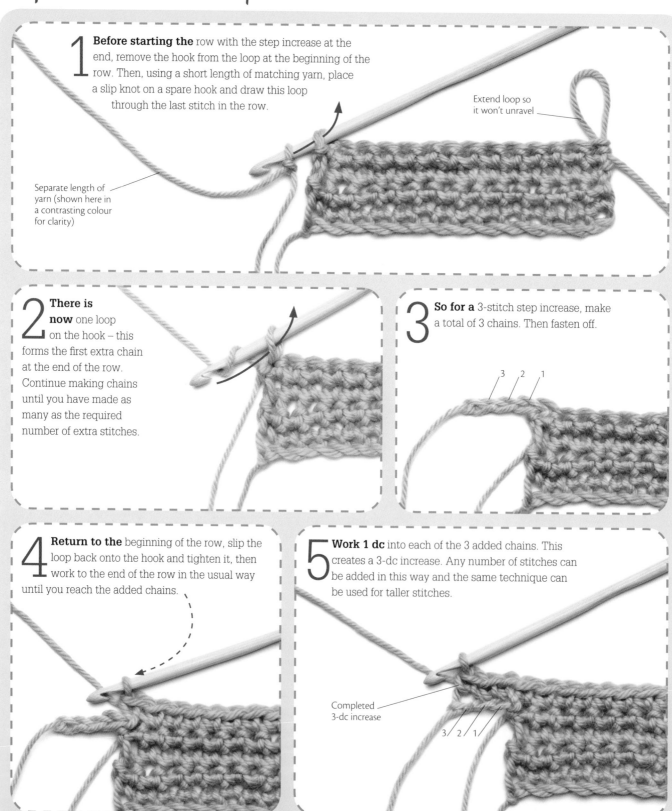

1 **Before starting the** row with the step increase at the end, remove the hook from the loop at the beginning of the row. Then, using a short length of matching yarn, place a slip knot on a spare hook and draw this loop through the last stitch in the row.

Extend loop so it won't unravel

Separate length of yarn (shown here in a contrasting colour for clarity)

2 **There is now** one loop on the hook – this forms the first extra chain at the end of the row. Continue making chains until you have made as many as the required number of extra stitches.

3 **So for a** 3-stitch step increase, make a total of 3 chains. Then fasten off.

3 2 1

4 **Return to the** beginning of the row, slip the loop back onto the hook and tighten it, then work to the end of the row in the usual way until you reach the added chains.

5 **Work 1 dc** into each of the 3 added chains. This creates a 3-dc increase. Any number of stitches can be added in this way and the same technique can be used for taller stitches.

Completed 3-dc increase

3 2 1

Double crochet decreases (abbreviation = dc2tog)

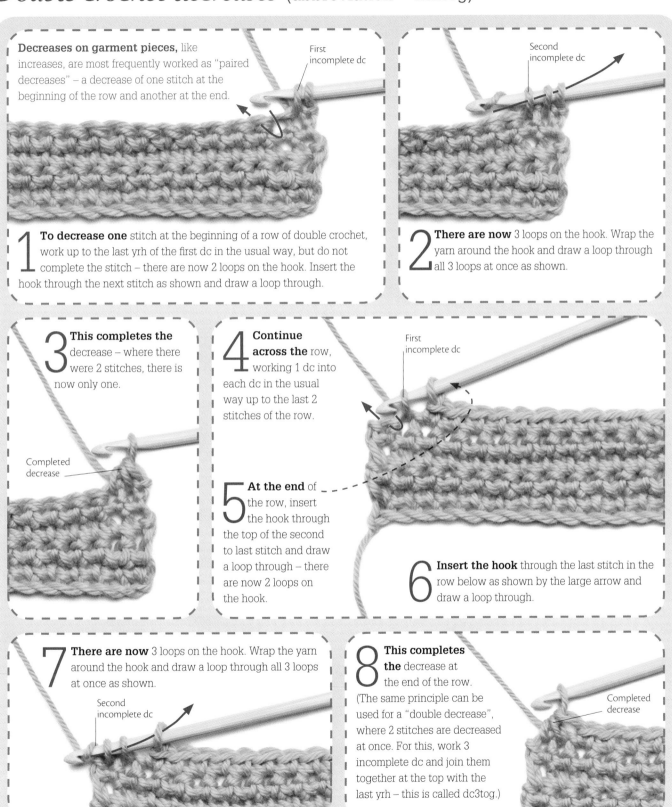

Decreases on garment pieces, like increases, are most frequently worked as "paired decreases" – a decrease of one stitch at the beginning of the row and another at the end.

First incomplete dc

Second incomplete dc

1 **To decrease one** stitch at the beginning of a row of double crochet, work up to the last yrh of the first dc in the usual way, but do not complete the stitch – there are now 2 loops on the hook. Insert the hook through the next stitch as shown and draw a loop through.

2 **There are now** 3 loops on the hook. Wrap the yarn around the hook and draw a loop through all 3 loops at once as shown.

3 **This completes the** decrease – where there were 2 stitches, there is now only one.

Completed decrease

4 **Continue across the** row, working 1 dc into each dc in the usual way up to the last 2 stitches of the row.

First incomplete dc

5 **At the end** of the row, insert the hook through the top of the second to last stitch and draw a loop through – there are now 2 loops on the hook.

6 **Insert the hook** through the last stitch in the row below as shown by the large arrow and draw a loop through.

7 **There are now** 3 loops on the hook. Wrap the yarn around the hook and draw a loop through all 3 loops at once as shown.

Second incomplete dc

8 **This completes the** decrease at the end of the row. (The same principle can be used for a "double decrease", where 2 stitches are decreased at once. For this, work 3 incomplete dc and join them together at the top with the last yrh – this is called dc3tog.)

Completed decrease

Treble crochet decreases (abbreviation = tr2tog)

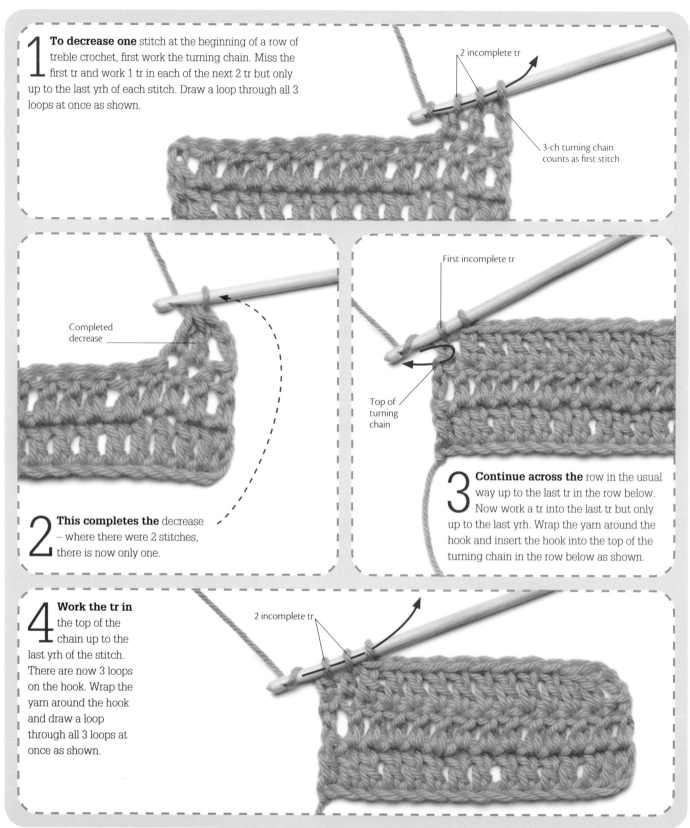

1 **To decrease one** stitch at the beginning of a row of treble crochet, first work the turning chain. Miss the first tr and work 1 tr in each of the next 2 tr but only up to the last yrh of each stitch. Draw a loop through all 3 loops at once as shown.

2 incomplete tr

3-ch turning chain counts as first stitch

Completed decrease

2 **This completes the** decrease – where there were 2 stitches, there is now only one.

First incomplete tr

Top of turning chain

3 **Continue across the** row in the usual way up to the last tr in the row below. Now work a tr into the last tr but only up to the last yrh. Wrap the yarn around the hook and insert the hook into the top of the turning chain in the row below as shown.

4 **Work the tr in** the top of the chain up to the last yrh of the stitch. There are now 3 loops on the hook. Wrap the yarn around the hook and draw a loop through all 3 loops at once as shown.

2 incomplete tr

5 **This completes the** decrease at the end of the row. (The same principle can be used for a "double decrease", where 2 stitches are decreased at once. For this, work 3 incomplete tr and join them together at the top with the last yrh – this is called tr3tog.)

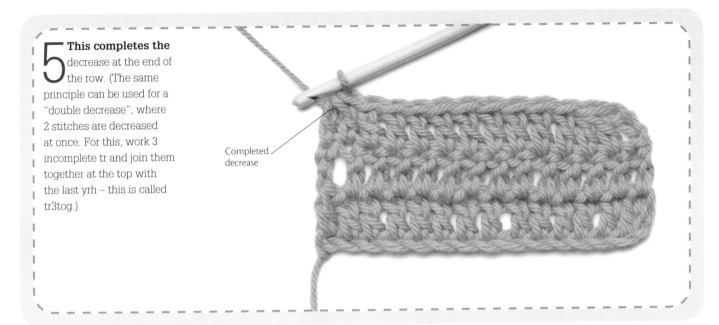

Completed decrease

Step decreases

1 **At beginning of row:** Decreases, like increases, can also be worked so that they form little steps at the edge. As an example, to decrease 3 stitches at the beginning of a row of double crochet, work 1 chain and then 1 slip stitch into each of the first 4 dc. Next, work 1 chain, then work the first dc in the same place that the last slip stitch was worked. Continue along the row in the usual way.

2 **At end of row:** For a 3-stitch step decrease at the end of the row, simply work up to the last 3 stitches at the end of the row and turn, leaving the last 3 stitches unworked. This technique can be used for all crochet stitches.

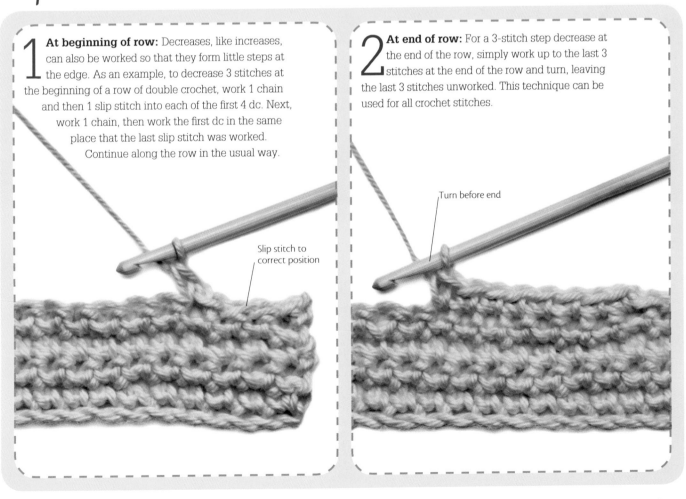

Slip stitch to correct position

Turn before end

Simple edging patterns

Adding a decorative crochet edging to an otherwise mundane-looking piece of crochet can transform it, giving it a touch of elegance. All the simple crochet edgings that follow are worked widthwise, so you start with a length of chain roughly equivalent to the length of edging you need. See p.35 for abbreviations.

Adding edgings

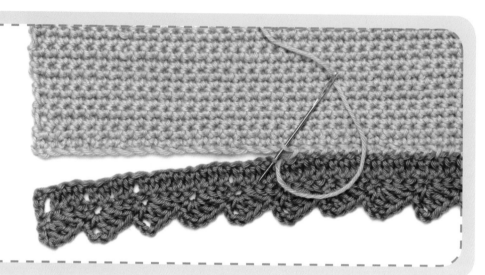

To sew an edging in place, use a yarn that matches the base crochet and a blunt-ended yarn needle. Secure the yarn at the right-hand end of the seam with 2 or 3 overcast stitches. Then work evenly spaced overcast stitches through both the base crochet and the edging, as shown.

Simple edging patterns

Grand eyelet edging

Make a multiple of 7 ch, plus 2 extra.

Row 1 (WS): 1 dc in 2nd ch from hook, 1 dc in each of rem ch. Turn.

Row 2 (RS): 1 ch, 1 dc in first dc, 1 htr in next dc, 1 tr in next dc, 1 dtr in next dc, *5 ch, miss next 3 dc, 1 dc in next dc, 1 htr in next dc, 1 tr in next dc, 1 dtr in next dc; rep from * to last 4 dc, 5 ch, miss next 3 dc, 1 dc in last dc.
Fasten off.

Suitable even for beginners, these edgings are perfect for dressing up towel ends, throws, baby blankets, necklines, and cuffs. When making an edging that will encircle a blanket, be sure to add extra for turning the corners; the edging can then be gathered at each corner to allow for the turning. Use a short test swatch to calculate how much extra you will need at each corner.

Triple picot edging

Make a multiple of 6 ch, plus 2 extra.

Row 1 (WS): 1 dc in 2nd ch from hook, 1 dc in each of rem ch. Turn.

Row 2 (RS): 5 ch, work [1 dc, (5 ch, 1 dc) twice] all in first dc, *4 ch, miss next 5 dc, [1 dc, (5 ch, 1 dc) 3 times] all in next dc; rep from * to end.
Fasten off.

Picot scallop edging

Make a multiple of 4 ch, plus 2 extra.

Row 1 (WS): 1 dc in 2nd ch from hook, *5 ch, miss next 3 ch, 1 dc in next ch; rep from * to end. Turn.

Row 2 (RS): 1 ch, *work [4 dc, 3 ch, 4 dc] all in next 5-ch loop; rep from * to end.
Fasten off.

Simple multiple-stitch edging

Make a multiple of 8 ch, plus 2 extra.

Row 1 (WS): 1 dc in 2nd ch from hook, 1 dc in each of rem ch. Turn.

Row 2 (RS): 1 ch, 1 ss in first dc, *1 dc in next dc, 1 htr in next dc, 1 tr in next dc; 3 dtr in next dc, 1 tr in next dc, 1 htr in next dc, 1 dc in next dc, 1 ss in next dc, rep from * to end.
Fasten off.

Simple shell edging

Make a multiple of 6 ch, plus 2 extra.

Row 1 (RS): 1 dc in 2nd ch from hook, 1 dc in each of rem ch. Turn.

Row 2: 5 ch, miss first 3 dc, 1 tr in next dc, *5 ch, miss next 5 dc, 1 tr in next dc; rep from * to last 3 dc, 2 ch, miss next 2 dc, 1 tr in last dc. Turn.

Row 3: 1 ch, 1 dc in first tr, 3 ch, 3 tr in next tr, *3 ch, 1 dc in next 5-ch space, 3 ch, 3 tr in next tr; rep from *, ending with 3 ch, miss first 2 ch of last 5-ch, 1 dc in next ch.
Fasten off.

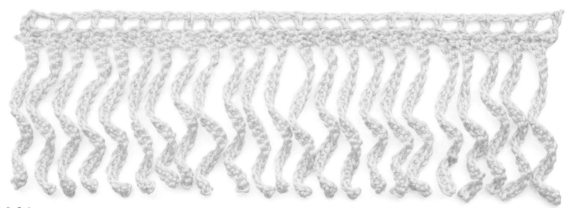

Twirl fringe

Note: The fringe will twirl naturally: do not press out the twirls.

To start edging, make a multiple of 2 ch.

Row 1 (WS): 1 dtr in 4th ch from hook, *1 ch, miss next ch, 1 dtr in next ch; rep from * to end. Turn.

Row 2 (RS): 1 ch, 1 dc in first dtr, *24 ch, 1 dc in 2nd ch from hook, 1 dc in each of rem 22 ch, 1 dc in next dtr; rep from * to end. **Fasten off.**

Double loop edging

To start edging, make a multiple of 5 ch, plus 2 extra.

Row 1 (WS): 1 dc in 2nd ch from hook, 1 dc in next ch, *5 ch, miss next 2 ch, 1 dc in each of next 3 ch; rep from * to last 4 ch, 5 ch, miss next 2 ch, 1 dc in each of last 2 ch. Turn.

Row 2 (RS): 1 ch, 1 dc in first dc, *8 ch, 1 dc in centre dc of next group of 3-dc (at other side of 5-ch loop); rep from * working last dc in last dc of row 1.
Fasten off.

Bold scallop edging

Make a multiple of 10 ch, plus 2 extra.

Row 1 (RS): 1 dc in 2nd ch from hook, 1 dc in each of rem ch. Turn.

Row 2: 1 ch, 1 dc in first dc, 2 ch, miss next 2 dc, 1 dc in next dc, 7 ch, miss next 3 dc, 1 dc in next dc, *6 ch, miss next 5 dc, 1 dc in next dc, 7 ch, miss next 3 dc, 1 dc in next dc; rep from * to last 3 dc, 2 ch, miss next 2 dc, 1 dc in last dc. Turn.

Row 3: 1 ch, 1 dc in first dc, 13 tr in 7-ch loop, *1 dc in next 6-ch sp, 13 tr in next 7-ch loop; rep from *, ending with 1 dc in last dc. **Fasten off.**

Cluster scallop edging

Make a multiple of 8 ch, plus 2 extra.

Row 1 (RS): 1 dc in 2nd ch from hook, 1 dc in each of rem ch. Turn.

Row 2: 1 ch, 1 dc in first dc, 1 dc in each of next 2 dc, *6 ch, miss next 3 dc, 1 dc in each of next 5 dc; rep from * to last 6 dc, 6 ch, miss next 3 dc, 1 dc in each of last 3 dc. Turn.

Row 3: 3 ch, work [yrh, insert hook in ch sp, yrh and draw a loop through, yrh and draw through first 2 loops on hook] 3 times in next 6-ch sp, 4 loops now on hook, yrh and draw through all 4 loops on hook to close 3-tr group (called 3-tr cluster), *4 ch, 3-tr cluster in same ch sp, 4 ch, 3-tr cluster in same ch sp BUT do not close cluster (leave last 4 loops on hook), 3-tr cluster in next 6-ch sp and close this cluster and last cluster at the same time by drawing a loop through all 7 loops on hook; rep from * to last 6-ch sp, [4 ch, 3-tr cluster in same ch sp] twice, 1 tr in last dc of row 2.
Fasten off.

Cluster and shell edging

Make a multiple of 8 ch, plus 4 extra.

Row 1 (WS): 1 tr in 4th ch from hook, *miss next 3 ch, 6 tr in next ch (to make a shell), miss next 3 ch, work [1 tr, 1 ch, 1 tr] all in next ch; rep from * to last 8 ch, miss next 3 ch, 6 tr in next ch, miss next 3 ch, 2 tr in last ch. Turn.

Row 2 (RS): 1 ch, miss first tr, 1 dc in next tr, *4 ch, [yrh, insert hook in next tr, yrh and draw a loop through, yrh and draw through first 2 loops on hook] 6 times (once into each of 6 tr of shell), yrh and draw through all 7 loops on hook to complete cluster, 6 ch, 1 ss in top of cluster just made, 4 ch, 1 dc in next 1-ch sp (between 2 tr); rep from * to end, working last dc of last rep in top of 3-ch at end.
Fasten off.

Step edging

Make a multiple of 4 ch, plus 3 extra.

Row 1 (WS): 1 tr in 4th ch from hook, 1 tr in each of rem ch. Turn.

Row 2 (RS): 3 ch, 3 tr in first tr, *miss next 3 tr, work [1 dc, 3 ch, 3 tr] all in next tr; rep from * to last 3 tr, miss last 3 tr, 1 dc in top of 3-ch at end.
Fasten off.

Bookmark

Worked in fine crochet cotton, this small project makes a lovely and quick gift. If you have never used crochet cotton and a small hook before, a bit of care and patience is required but the results are stunning. Press the bookmark lightly once finished to flatten it.

essential info ...

SIZE
2cm x 18cm (¾in x 7in)

YARN
A: DMC Petra 100g x 1

A

CROCHET HOOK
1.5mm hook

NOTIONS
Yarn needle

Bookmark
Work 51 ch.

Row 1: Miss 1 ch, dc in each rem ch to end. (50sts)

Rows 2–3: 1 ch, turn. Dc in each dc to end. (50sts)

Row 4: 1 ch, turn. Dc in first st, *miss 1st, 5 tr in next st, miss 1st, ss in next st; rep from * around entire piece including other side of foundation chain, ending dc in last st, leaving last short side unworked.

Fasten off, weave in ends.

Tassel
Cut 8 lengths of cotton twice the length of your desired tassel (the sample used lengths of 40cm/16in). Insert hook into centre of unworked short side, fold cotton lengths over hook at centre of lengths, pull loop through, fold all tails over hook and pull tails through. Trim neatly.

A tassel is surprisingly easy to make. It provides a neat finishing touch and makes it easy to find your place in the book.

Shell edging runs along both sides of the bookmark, giving the appearance of a symmetrical pattern.

Shawl

This lacy, feminine shawl uses a variation of the chain loop mesh stitch (see p.66) as well as the picot and shell edgings (see p.87). The shawl is made in rows, starting with the longest row at the top and decreasing naturally down to a point at the bottom.

essential info ...

SIZE
135cm x 105cm (53in x 41in)

YARN
A: Sirdar Balmoral DK 50g x 5

A

CROCHET HOOK
4.5mm hook

NOTIONS
Yarn needle

Shawl

Work 181 ch (or any multiple of 3+1).

Row 1: Miss first ch, dc in each ch to end. Turn. (180sts)

Row 2: *6 ch, miss 2 sts, dc in next st; rep from * to end. Turn.

Row 3 and all following rows: Ss in first 3 chs, *6 ch, dc in next 6-ch loop; rep from * to end. Turn. Rep last row until left with one 6-ch loop.

Fasten off, weave in ends.

TOP PICOT EDGING

Working along top of shawl, attach yarn at one end, 1 ch, dc in same st, *4 ch, ss in 4th ch from hook, dc in each of next 2 sts; rep from * across top edge, ending (4 ch, ss in 4th ch from hook, dc) all in last st. Leave yarn attached.

SIDE SHELL EDGING

Working around two remaining sides, *ss in next 6-ch loop, 5 tr in same sp, ss in same sp; rep from * around two un-edged sides, working (ss, 10 tr, ss) in loop at bottom point.

Fasten off, weave in ends.

Shell edging finishes the long sides of the shawl. Each shell in the edging matches up with a single space in the lace pattern.

tips ...

Picot edging is used to finish the top of the shawl. The edging can be made larger by adding chains.

The shawl curls naturally around the neck and
will stay put on the shoulders.

Wrist warmers

Lacy and pretty yet surprisingly warm, this simple wrist warmer pattern works up quickly, and the softly variegated yarn provides visual appeal. This project is finished with a variation of the picot scallop edging (see p.87).

(see p.87)

essential info ...

SIZE
To fit an adult female

YARN
A: Rowan Creative Focus 100g x 1

A

CROCHET HOOK
5mm hook

NOTIONS
Yarn needle

TENSION
3.5 pattern repeats per 10cm (4in)

Wrist warmers (Make 2)
Work 28 ch (loosely).

Row 1: Dc in 2nd ch from hook, 3 ch, miss next ch, 1 tr in next ch, *2 ch, miss next ch, 1 dc in next ch, 2 ch, miss next ch, 1 tr in next ch; rep from * to end. Turn.

Row 2: 1 ch, 1 dc in first tr, 2 ch, 1 tr in next dc, *2 ch, 1 dc in next tr, 2 ch, 1 tr in next dc; rep from * to end. Turn.

Rep row 2 until piece measures 17cm (7in). Do not fasten off.

TOP EDGING
1 ch, dc in first tr. Work [2 dc, 3 ch, 2 dc] in each 2-ch sp to end, dc in last dc. Do not fasten off.

Finishing
Ss join down open sides (see p.121), leaving 4cm (1½in), or length desired, open for thumb hole. When sides are joined, 2 ch and work htr around entire lower edge of piece.

(see p.121)

Fasten off, weave in ends.

tips ...

Picot edging along the top of each wrist warmer adds a pretty finishing touch.

The thumb hole is formed by leaving a gap of around 4cm (1½in) between the two seams when the two sides of the crocheted square are joined together.

Wrist warmer can be left as is or turned inside out to hide seam, as desired.

Circular crochet

Crochet can be worked not only back and forth in rows, but round and round in circles to form tubes or flat shapes started from the centre (called medallions). The basic techniques for crocheting in the round are very easy to learn, even for a beginner, so it is not surprising that many popular crochet accessories are made with circular crochet, including flowers and afghan motifs, as well as seamless toys, hats, mittens, containers, and bags.

Starting a tube

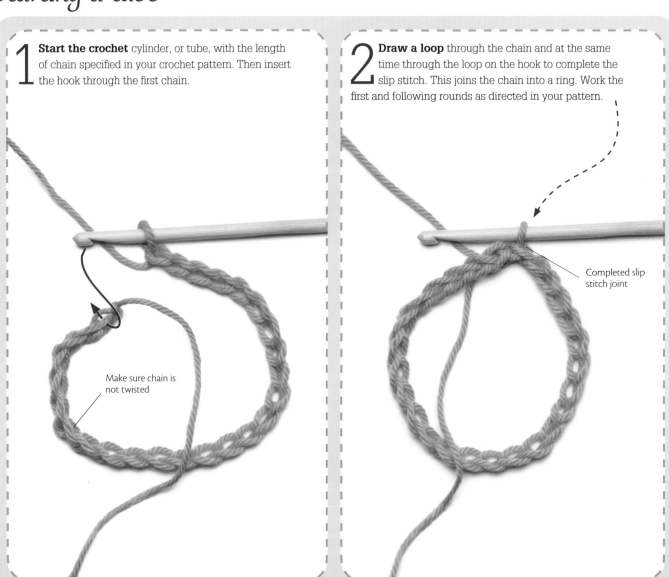

1 **Start the crochet** cylinder, or tube, with the length of chain specified in your crochet pattern. Then insert the hook through the first chain.

Make sure chain is not twisted

2 **Draw a loop** through the chain and at the same time through the loop on the hook to complete the slip stitch. This joins the chain into a ring. Work the first and following rounds as directed in your pattern.

Completed slip stitch joint

Double crochet spiral tubes

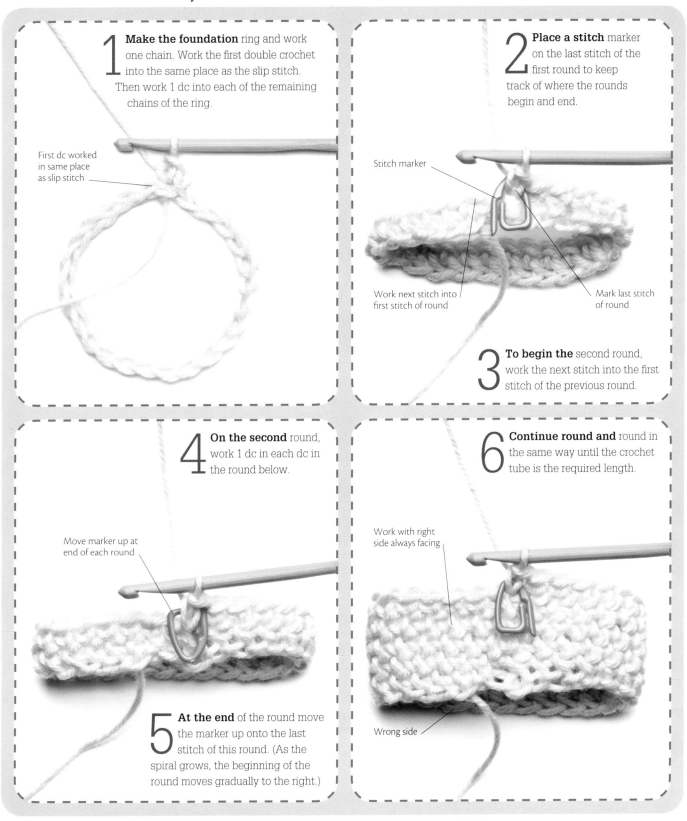

1 **Make the foundation** ring and work one chain. Work the first double crochet into the same place as the slip stitch. Then work 1 dc into each of the remaining chains of the ring.

First dc worked in same place as slip stitch

2 **Place a stitch** marker on the last stitch of the first round to keep track of where the rounds begin and end.

Stitch marker

Work next stitch into first stitch of round

Mark last stitch of round

3 **To begin the** second round, work the next stitch into the first stitch of the previous round.

4 **On the second** round, work 1 dc in each dc in the round below.

Move marker up at end of each round

5 **At the end** of the round move the marker up onto the last stitch of this round. (As the spiral grows, the beginning of the round moves gradually to the right.)

6 **Continue round and** round in the same way until the crochet tube is the required length.

Work with right side always facing

Wrong side

Treble crochet tube without turns

When basic stitches taller than double crochet are used to make crochet tubes, each round is started with a turning chain.

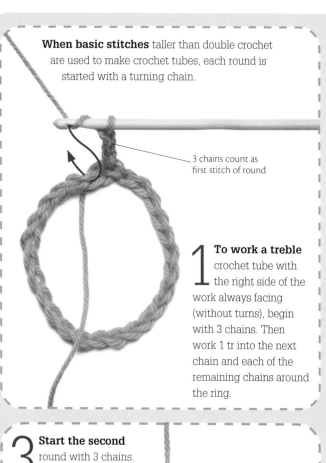

3 chains count as first stitch of round

1 **To work a treble** crochet tube with the right side of the work always facing (without turns), begin with 3 chains. Then work 1 tr into the next chain and each of the remaining chains around the ring.

2 **At the end** of the round, join the last stitch to the top of the turning chain at the beginning of the round by working a slip stitch into the third of the 3 chains.

Join with a slip stitch to top of 3 chains

3 **Start the second** round with 3 chains. There is no need to mark the end of the round with a stitch marker as the turning chain shows where each round begins. Continue around the tube again, working 1 tr into each tr in the previous round.

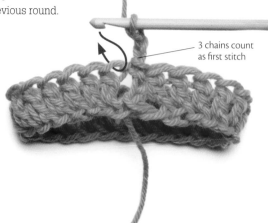

3 chains count as first stitch

4 **At the end** of the second round, join the last stitch to the top of the turning chain with a slip stitch. Continue in the same way, beginning all following rounds with 3 chains.

Right side shows fronts of trebles

Wrong side shows back of trebles

Treble crochet tube with turns

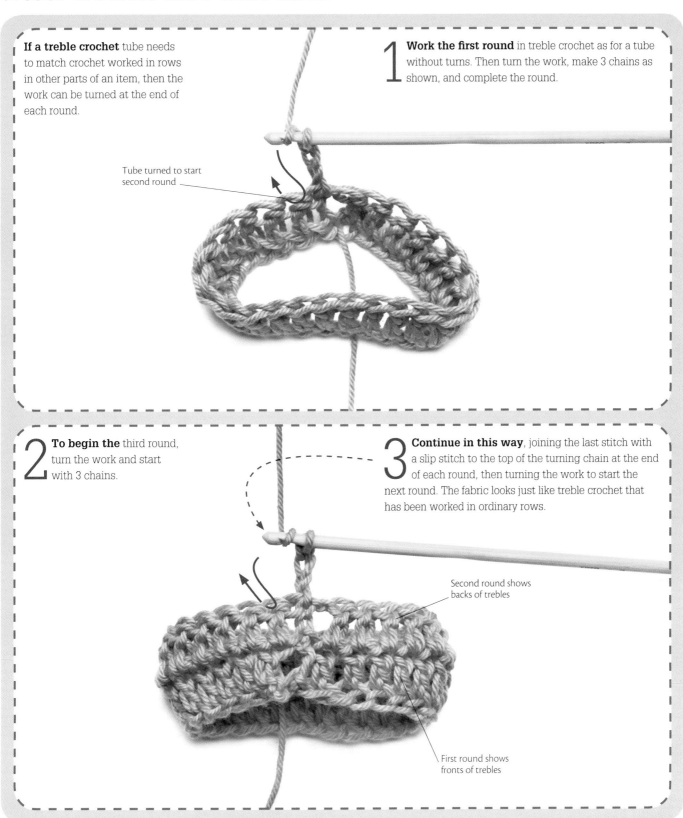

If a treble crochet tube needs to match crochet worked in rows in other parts of an item, then the work can be turned at the end of each round.

1 **Work the first round** in treble crochet as for a tube without turns. Then turn the work, make 3 chains as shown, and complete the round.

Tube turned to start second round

2 **To begin the** third round, turn the work and start with 3 chains.

3 **Continue in this way**, joining the last stitch with a slip stitch to the top of the turning chain at the end of each round, then turning the work to start the next round. The fabric looks just like treble crochet that has been worked in ordinary rows.

Second round shows backs of trebles

First round shows fronts of trebles

Flat circles

Making a simple circle is a good example for how other flat medallion shapes are started and then worked round and round from the centre. The circle is also used in conjunction with the crochet tube to make parts of toys (see pp.102–103 and 106–109) or containers (see pp.104–105), so it is well worth practising.

Making a flat circle

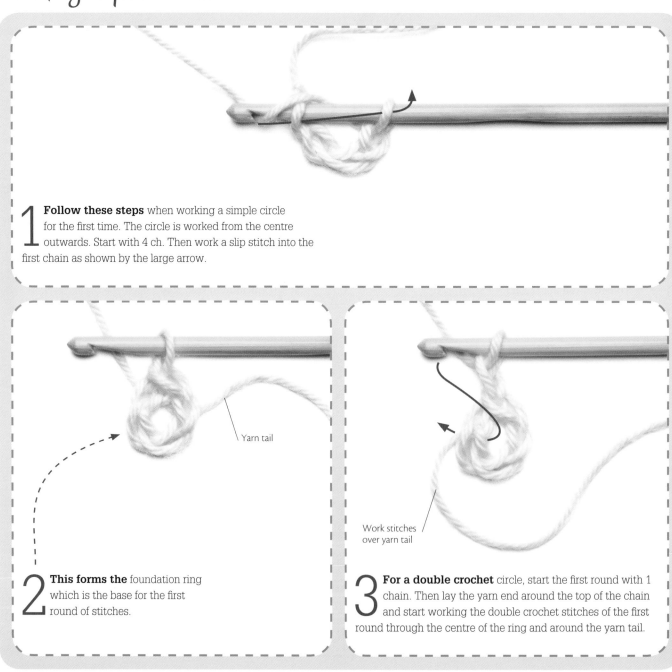

1 **Follow these steps** when working a simple circle for the first time. The circle is worked from the centre outwards. Start with 4 ch. Then work a slip stitch into the first chain as shown by the large arrow.

Yarn tail

2 **This forms the** foundation ring which is the base for the first round of stitches.

Work stitches over yarn tail

3 **For a double crochet** circle, start the first round with 1 chain. Then lay the yarn end around the top of the chain and start working the double crochet stitches of the first round through the centre of the ring and around the yarn tail.

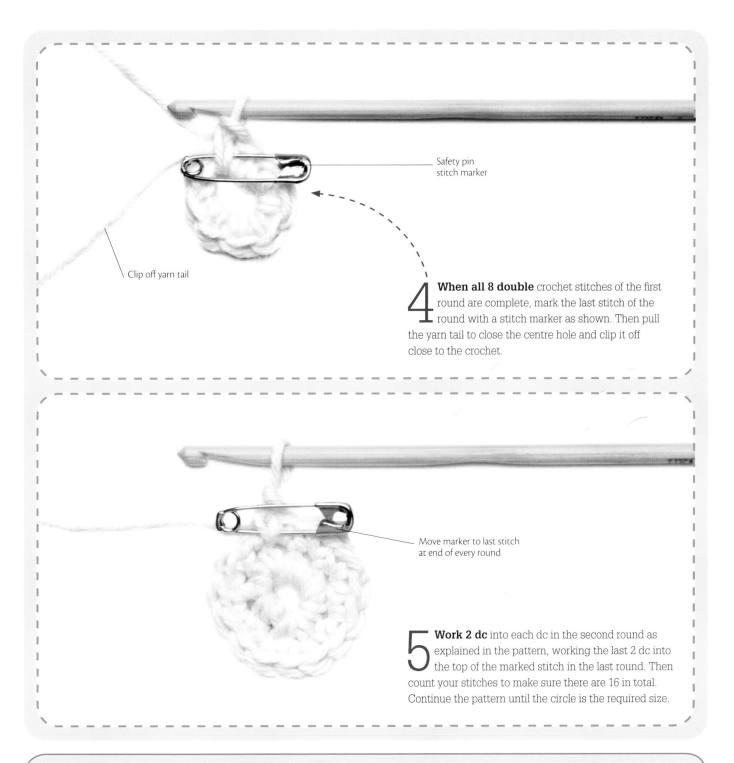

Safety pin
stitch marker

Clip off yarn tail

4 **When all 8 double** crochet stitches of the first
round are complete, mark the last stitch of the
round with a stitch marker as shown. Then pull
the yarn tail to close the centre hole and clip it off
close to the crochet.

Move marker to last stitch
at end of every round

5 **Work 2 dc** into each dc in the second round as
explained in the pattern, working the last 2 dc into
the top of the marked stitch in the last round. Then
count your stitches to make sure there are 16 in total.
Continue the pattern until the circle is the required size.

Alternative methods for working flat circles

2-chain: Start with 2 ch. Work required number of dc into 2nd ch from hook, then ss in first dc to close.

Magic loop: Make a loop with yarn (do not start with slip stitch). Insert hook into loop and pull working yarn through. 1 ch. Working under both loop and tail, insert hook into loop and make required number of dc. Then pull tail to close loop.

Teddy bear

This adorable teddy is made in continuous rounds. The head is started from the top and the body from the bottom; both are decreased to the same number of stitches and then stuffed and joined. Arms, legs, and ears are added separately, as is a contrasting scarf for the perfect finishing touch.

essential info ...

SIZE
15cm (6in)

YARN
A: Stylecraft Special DK 100g x 1
B: Rowan Purelife DK 50g x 1

A   B

CROCHET HOOK
A: 3mm hook (for teddy)
B: 4mm hook (for scarf)

NOTIONS
Toy stuffing
Brown and black embroidery thread
Yarn needle

Teddy bear
HEAD (Make 2)
Make 6 dc in magic loop (see p.101), pull tail to close.

Round 1: 2 dc in each dc to end. (12sts)
Round 2: *1 dc in next dc, 2 dc in next dc; rep from * to end. (18sts)
Round 3: *1 dc in each of next 2 dc, 2 dc in next dc; rep from * to end. (24sts)
Round 4: *1 dc in each of next 3 dc, 2 dc in next dc; rep from * to end. (30sts)
Round 5: *1 dc in each of next 4 dc, 2 dc in next dc; rep from * to end. (36sts)
Round 6: *1 dc in each of next 5 dc, 2 dc in next dc; rep from * to end. (42sts)
Rounds 7–14: 1 dc in each dc to end. (42sts)
Round 15: *1 dc in each of next 5 dc, dc2tog; rep from * to end. (36sts)

Round 16: *1 dc in each of next 4 dc, dc2tog; rep from * to end. (30sts)
Round 17: *1 dc in each of next 3 dc, dc2tog; rep from * to end. (24sts)

Fasten off, leaving a long tail.

EARS (Make 2)
Make 5 dc in magic loop, pull tail to close.

Round 1: 2 dc in each dc to end. (10sts)
Rounds 2–3: 1 dc in each dc to end. (10sts)

Fasten off, leaving a long tail.

BODY
Make 6 dc in magic loop, pull tail to close.

Round 1: 2 dc in each dc to end. (12sts)
Round 2: *1 dc in next dc, 2 dc in next dc; rep from * to end. (18sts)
Round 3: *1 dc in each of next 2 dc, 2 dc in next dc; rep from * to end. (24sts)
Round 4: *1 dc in each of next 3 dc, 2 dc in next dc; rep from * to end. (30sts)
Round 5: *1 dc in each of next 4 dc, 2 dc in next dc; rep from * to end. (36sts)
Round 6: *1 dc in each of next 5 dc, 2 dc in next dc; rep from * to end. (42sts)
Rounds 7–14: 1 dc in each dc to end. (42sts)
Round 15: *1 dc in each of next 5 dc, dc2tog; rep from * to end. (36sts)
Rounds 16–17: 1 dc in each dc to end. (36sts)
Round 18: *1 dc in each of next 4 dc, dc2tog; rep from * to end. (30sts)
Rounds 19–20: 1 dc in each dc to end. (30sts)
Round 21: *1 dc in each of next 3 dc, dc2tog; rep from * to end. (24sts)
Rounds 22–23: 1 dc in each dc to end. (24sts)

Fasten off, leaving a long tail.

LEGS (Make 2)
Make 6 dc in magic loop, pull tail to close.

Round 1: 2 dc in each dc to end. (12sts)
Round 2: *1 dc in next dc, 2 dc in next dc; rep from * to end. (18sts)
Round 3: *1 dc in each of next 2 dc, 2 dc in next dc; rep from * to end. (24sts)
Round 4: *1 dc in each of next 3 dc, 2 dc in next dc; rep from * to end. (30sts)
Round 5: dc2tog to end. (15sts)
Rounds 6–9: 1 dc in each dc to end. (15sts)

Fasten off, leaving a long tail.

ARMS (Make 2)
Make 6 dc in magic loop, pull tail to close

Round 1: 2 dc in each dc to end. (12sts)
Rounds 2–8: 1 dc in each dc to end. (12sts)

Fasten off, leaving a long tail.

Scarf
Work 31 ch.

Row 1: Miss 1 dc, dc in rem 30 chs. (30sts)
Row 2: 1 ch, dc in each dc to end.

Fasten off, weave in ends.

Finishing
Embroider eyes, nose, and mouth on to the head piece and then stuff firmly. Use the long tail on the ears to sew the open ends to the head. Stuff the body firmly and sew it to the head. Then stuff the legs and arms and use the long tails to stitch them to the body. Tie the scarf around the teddy's neck.

The head and neck are both worked to the same number of stitches, and attached to each other with matching yarn.

The teddy's eyes, nose, and mouth are embroidered on the finished head with black and brown embroidery thread.

Project basket

This handy, versatile basket is made in the round, starting at the centre bottom. The bottom edge and brim fold are cleverly made by crocheting only into the back loop of the stitch for one round.

essential info ...

SIZE
13cm x 16cm (5in x 6in)

YARN
A: Stylecraft Special DK 100g x 1
B: Stylecraft Special DK 100g x 1

A   B

CROCHET HOOK
4mm hook

NOTIONS
Yarn needle

Basket

With yarn A, work 2 ch, 6 dc in 2nd ch from hook.

Round 1: 2 dc in each dc to end. (12sts)
Round 2: *1 dc in next dc, 2 dc in next dc; rep from * to end. (18sts)
Round 3: *1 dc in each of next 2 dc, 2 dc in next dc; rep from * to end. (24sts)
Round 4: *1 dc in each of next 3 dc, 2 dc in next dc; rep from * to end. (30sts)
Round 5: *1 dc in each of next 4 dc, 2 dc in next dc; rep from * to end. (36sts)
Round 6: *1 dc in each of next 5 dc, 2 dc in next dc; rep from * to end. (42sts)
Round 7: *1 dc in each of next 6 dc, 2 dc in next dc; rep from * to end. (48sts)
Round 8: *1 dc in each of next 7 dc, 2 dc in next dc; rep from * to end. (54sts)
Round 9: *1 dc in each of next 8 dc, 2 dc in next dc; rep from * to end. (60sts)
Round 10: *1 dc in each of next 9 dc, 2 dc in next dc; rep from * to end. (66sts)
Round 11: *1 dc in each of next 10 dc, 2 dc in next dc; rep from * to end. (72sts)
Round 12: *1 dc in each of next 11 dc, 2 dc in next dc; rep from * to end. (78sts)
Round 13: *1 dc in each of next 12 dc, 2 dc in next dc; rep from * to end. (84sts)
Round 14: *1 dc in each of next 13 dc, 2 dc in next dc; rep from * to end. (90sts)
Round 15: *1 dc in each of next 14 dc, 2 dc in next dc; rep from * to end. (96sts)
Round 16: *1 dc in each of next 15 dc, 2 dc in next dc; rep from * to end. (102sts)
Increase can be stopped earlier for a smaller basket or continued as set for a larger basket

Round 17: Working into back loops only, dc in each dc to end. (102sts)
Cont working even rounds through both loops (1 dc in each dc to end) until piece measures 13cm (5in) from Round 17, or desired height.

FOLDOVER
Round 1: Working in the front loops only, with yarn B, 1 dc in each dc to end. (102sts)
Round 2: With yarn A, 1 dc in each dc through both loops to end. (102sts)
Round 3: With yarn B, 1 dc in each dc through both loops to end. (102sts)
Rep last 2 rounds once more.

Fasten off, weave in ends.

As rounds increase on the bottom of the basket, it begins to look more and more like a hexagon.

The decorative brim with three
contrasting stripes is crocheted
as part of the basket and then
folded down.

Size can be adjusted by
adding or subtracting increase
and even rounds.

Toy dog

Although crocheted toys look difficult, they are very easy to make, and quick as well. Be very careful if you are making any toy for a small child that they are safe to play with – it is best to embroider the eyes or select toy safety eyes that meet safety regulations.

essential info ...

SIZE
30cm (12in)

YARN
A: Rowan Sienna 4-ply 50g x 2
B: Rowan Sienna 4-ply 50g x 1
C: Rowan Sienna 4-ply 50g x 1
D: Rowan Sienna 4-ply 50g x 1
E: Rowan Sienna 4-ply 50g x 1

A   B   C   D   E

CROCHET HOOK
2mm hook

NOTIONS
Six-stranded cotton embroidery
   thread (eyebrows, nose, and mouth)
Toy stuffing
Button eyes or toy safety eyes
Yarn needle

Special notes

When changing to a new colour, introduce the new colour by using it for the last yrh at the end of the previous round.

Do not cut off A and C when they are not in use, but drop them inside the piece until they are needed again. Begin and end B in the rows it is needed.

Toy

BODY AND HEAD

The body and head are worked in one piece in spiral dc, starting at the lower end of the body.

Using A, work 28 ch and join with a ss to first ch to form a ring, leaving a long loose end for sewing on legs later.

Round 1 (RS): 1 ch (does NOT count as a st), 1 dc in same place as ss, 1 dc in each of rem ch. 28 dc. (Do not turn at end of rounds but work in a spiral with RS always facing.)
Note: Mark last st of round 1 with a safety pin and move this marker onto last st at end of every round.

Begin the stripe sequence of [3 rounds A, 1 round B, 1 round C, 2 rounds A, 1 round C], which is repeated throughout, **and at the same time** cont shaping body as follows:

Round 2: [2 dc in next dc, I dc in each of next 6 de] 4 times. 32 dc.
Round 3: 1 dc in each dc to end of round.
Round 4: [1 dc in each of next 3 dc, 2 dc in next de] 8 times. 40 dc.
Round 5: Rep round 3.
Round 6: [1 dc in each of next 9 dc, 2 dc in next dc] 4 times. 44 dc.
Rounds 7–12: [Rep round 3] 6 times.
Round 13: [1 dc in each of next 9 dc, dc2tog 14 times. 40 dc.
Round 14: 1 dc in each of next 4 dc, [dc2tog, 1 dc in each of next 8 dc] 3 times, dc2tog, 1 dc in each of next 4 dc. 36 dc.
Round 15: [1 dc in each of next 7 dc, dc2tog] 4 times. 32 dc.
Round 16: Rep round 3.
Round 17: 1 dc in each of next 3 dc, [dc2tog, 1 dc in each of next 6 de] 3 times, dc2tog, 1 dc in each of next 3 dc. 28 dc.
Rounds 18–24: [Rep round 3] 7 times.

Shape neck and head
Round 25: [1 dc in each of next 5 dc, dc2tog] 4 times. 24 dc.

Round 26: [1 dc in next dc, dc2tog] 8 times. 16 dc.
Round 27: Rep round 3.
Round 28: [1 dc in next dc, 2 dc in next de] 8 times. 24 dc.
Round 29: 1 dc in each of next 3 dc, 2 dc in next de] 6 times. 30 dc.
Round 30: 1 dc in each of next 4 dc, 2 dc in next de] 6 times. 36 dc.
Rounds 31–39: [Rep round 3] 9 times, marking centre of rounds 37 and 38 with a coloured thread when they are reached (for position of eyes).
Round 40: [1 dc in each of next 4 dc, dc2tog] 6 times. 30 dc.

Using a strong button thread, sew on eyes now (or attach safety eyes), positioning them over rounds 37 and 38 in the centre of the rounds and about 12mm/½in apart. Then complete head as follows:-

Round 41: Rep round 3.
Cut off C and cont with A only.
Round 42: [1 dc in each of next 3 dc, dc2tog] 6 times. 24 dc.
Round 43: Rep round 3.
Round 44: [1 dc in next dc, dc2tog] 8 times. 16 dc.
Round 45: [Dc2tog] 8 times. 8 dc.

Fasten off, leaving a long loose end.

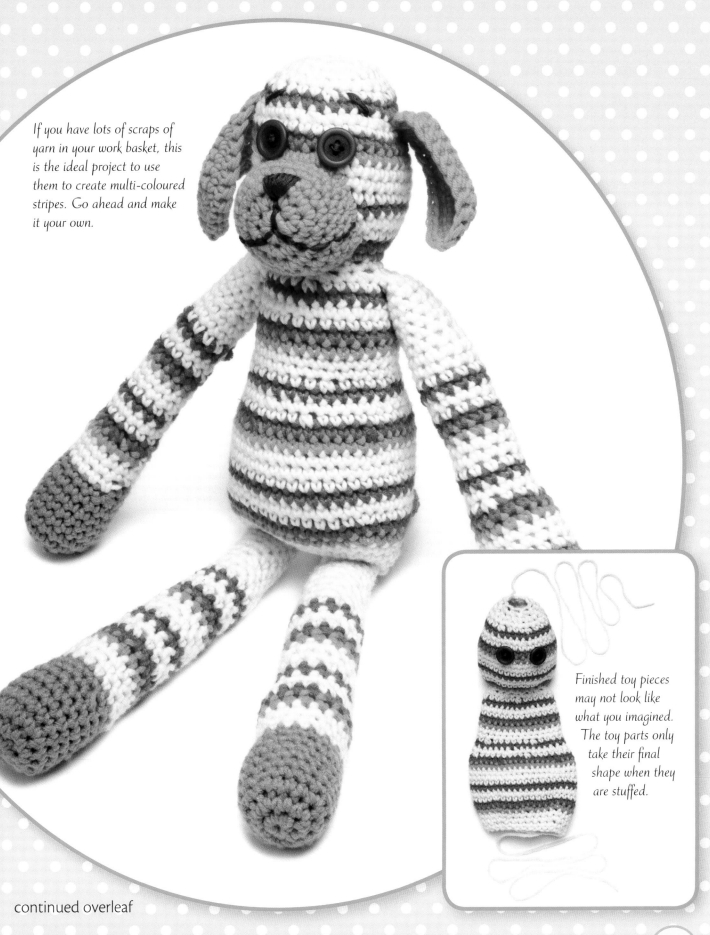

If you have lots of scraps of yarn in your work basket, this is the ideal project to use them to create multi-coloured stripes. Go ahead and make it your own.

Finished toy pieces may not look like what you imagined. The toy parts only take their final shape when they are stuffed.

continued overleaf

tips ...

A long loose end is often left at the top of the legs and arms – this is used to sew their tops closed. If you happen to leave a yarn end that is too short, join on a new length of yarn, but it is easier to use a strand already attached to the crochet.

LEGS (Make 2)
Each leg is started at the foot end.

Using D, make a loop ring by forming a circle with the yarn and drawing a loop through it with the hook (see p.101), then begin as follows:

Round 1 (RS): 1 ch (does NOT count as a st). 8 dc in loop ring. (Do not turn at end of rounds, but work with RS always facing.)
Pull yarn end to close loop ring.
Note: Mark last st of round 1 with a safety pin and move this marker onto last st at end of every round.
Round 2: [2 dc in next de] 8 times. 16 dc.**
Round 3: [1 dc in each of next 3 dc, 2 dc in next dc] 4 times. 20 dc.
Before proceeding, pull yarn end at beg of foot again and darn it in securely on WS.
Round 4: 1 dc in each to end of round.
Rounds 5–7: [Rep round 4] 3 times.
Round 8: [1 dc in each of next 3 dc, dc2tog] 4 times. 16 dc.
Round 9: Rep round 4.

This completes the foot.

Begin stripe sequence
Begin repeated stripe sequence as for body and at the same time cont leg as follows:

Rounds 10–14: [Rep round 4] 5 times.
Round 15: [1 dc in each of next 2 dc, dc2tog] 4 times. 12 dc.
Rounds 16–25: [Rep round 4] 10 times.

Cut off D and cont with A only.
Rounds 26–28: [Rep round 4] 3 times.

Round 29: [Dc2tog. 1 dc in each of next 4 dc twice. 10 dc.
Rounds 30–34: [Rep round 4] 5 times.

Work 1 ss in next dc and fasten off, leaving a long loose end.

ARMS (Make 2)
Make 2 arms in exactly same way as legs.

MUZZLE
Using E throughout, work as for leg to **.

Round 3: [1 dc in next dc. 2 dc in next de] 8 times. 24 dc.
Before proceeding, pull yarn end at beg of muzzle again and darn it in securely on WS.
Round 4: 1 dc in each to end of round.
Rounds 5–7: [Rep round 4] 3 times.

Work 1 ss in next dc and fasten off, leaving a long loose end for sewing muzzle to head.

EARS (Make 2)
Using E, work 10 ch.

Row 1 (WS): Working into only one loop of each foundation chain, work 1 dc in 2nd ch from hook, 1 dc in each of next 7 ch, 2 dc in last dc, then cont working around other side of foundation ch (working into other loop of each ch) as follows – 1 dc in first ch (same ch last 2-dc group was worked but on other side of this ch), 1 dc in each of rem 8 ch on this side of ch. Turn. 19 dc.

Row 2 (RS): 1 ch (does NOT count as a st), 1 dc in each of first 9 dc, 3 dc in next dc, 1 dc in each of rem 9 dc. Turn. 21 dc.

Row 3: 1 ch (does NOT count as a st), I dc in each of first 10 dc, 3 dc in next dc, 1 dc in each of rem 10 dc. Turn. 23 dc.

Row 4: 1 ch (does NOT count as a st), 1 dc in each of first 11 dc, work [1 dc. 2 ch. 1 dc] all in next dc, 1 dc in each of rem 11 dc.

Fasten off, leaving a long loose end for sewing on ear.

TAIL
Using E, work 14 ch.

Row 1: 1 tr in 4th ch from hook. 1 tr in each of rem ch.

Fasten off. (Tail will twirl naturally – do not press out this twirl.)

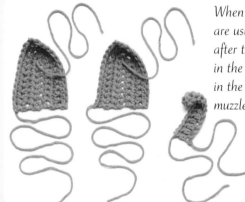

When making stuffed toys, there are usually other items to make after the main body. Crochet them in the order in which they appear in the pattern. In this pattern, the muzzle is crocheted before the two ears and tail, shown here.

The best stitch for long mouths on toys is backstitch. Position the centre of the dog's mouth in the centre hole of the muzzle. You can always unpick and redo stitching if you aren't satisfied with the facial features.

Leave the toy's eyebrows till last. These give your toy its unique expression. For each of the dog's eyebrows, work two stitches in the same place, on top of each other. Try different slants for different expressions.

Finishing

Using a yarn needle and the long loose end at the top of the head, gather the 8 dc of the last round and close the hole. Weave in all ends.

STUFFING AND TOY ASSEMBLING

Fill the toy's legs and arms. Push the toy filling in through the top of the leg and down towards the foot. Pinch together the top of each arm and leg, then use the long loose end to sew the top closed with overcast stitches. Don't trim off the loose ends. Pinch together the back and the front of the lower edge of the body, and pin at the centre. Using overcast stitches, sew the lower body seam between the legs, then sew the legs in place, followed by the arms. For the tail, darn in one of the yarn ends on the dog's tail and use the other to sew it to the body with overcast stitches. Stuff the muzzle and sew it in place with overcast stitches, pulling the stitches tight so they disappear.

ADDING FACIAL FEATURES

Use six-strand embroidery thread, doubled if necessary, and work the dog's nose in satin stitch. Then stitch the mouth in backstitch. For each ear, darn in the foundation-chain yarn end, then use the long loose end to gather the ear base to form a slightly cupped shape. Sew on the ears and then stitch the dog's eyebrows.

tips ...

Sew the dog's ears on to each side of the head so they are positioned at a slight diagonal. Fold them forwards after they are secure. To encourage ears into the correct shape, you can press them with steam.

Baby's booties

These adorable booties are made in the softest yarn for delicate skin, and in a style that is sure to stay on small feet. The booties are made in the round, starting with the sole. Be sure to use a stitch marker throughout to mark the first stitch of the round (see p.97).

essential info ...

SIZE
To fit a newborn baby

YARN
A: Sublime Cashmere Merino Silk DK 50g x 1

A

CROCHET HOOK
4mm hook

TENSION
Measure tension after completing the sole of each bootie. The length of the sole should be a minimum of 8.5cm (3¼in).

NOTIONS
4 small buttons
Yarn needle

Booties (Make 2)

Work 9 ch.

Round 1: Miss 1 ch, dc in each ch to end, 4 dc in last ch. Working down other side of ch, dc in each ch to end, work 4 dc in last ch. (22sts)

Round 2: *Dc in next 7 sts, work (1 dc in next st, 2 dc in next st) twice; rep from * once more. (26sts)

Round 3: *Dc in next 7 sts, work (1 dc in each of next 2 sts, 2 dc in next st) twice; rep from * once more. (30sts)

Round 4: *Dc in next 7 sts, work (1 dc in each of next 3 sts, 2 dc in next st) twice; rep from * once more. (34sts)

Round 5: Working into back loops only, dc in each dc to end. (34sts)

Round 6: Dc in next 7 sts, work (1 dc in each of next 3 sts, dc2tog) twice, dc in next 17 sts. (32sts)

Round 7: Dc in next 7 sts, tr2tog 4 times, dc in next 7 sts, htr in next 10 sts. (28sts)

Round 8: Dc in next 7 sts, tr2tog twice, dc in next 7 sts, htr in next 10 sts, ss in first st to close. (26sts)
Do not fasten off yarn.

The button loop at the end of each strap needs to fit snugly around the button. Adjust the size by adding or subtracting chains.

First strap: 9 ch, dc in 4th ch from hook and in each of next 5 chs, ss in beg st.

Fasten off.

Second strap: Rejoin yarn on other side of bootie at corresponding st (the last dc before the htr sts) and rep instructions for first strap.

Fasten off, weave in ends.

Attach buttons securely, as shown in picture.

The sole of the bootie is worked in rounds without joining. Be sure to check the measurement of each sole for tension.

The unusual crossed straps on these booties
will ensure they stay firmly on tiny feet.

Toy balls

These colourful little balls are made with small amounts of 4-ply mercerized cotton, and are a great way to use up leftover yarn. This project uses an especially small hook to achieve a tight tension, essential for making a solid fabric that will hold in the filling.

essential info ...

SIZE
5cm (2in) diameter

YARN
A: Rowan Siena 4-ply 50g x 1
B: Rowan Siena 4-ply 50g x 1
C: Rowan Siena 4-ply 50g x 1

A   B   C

CROCHET HOOK
2mm hook

NOTIONS
Toy stuffing
Yarn needle

Centre striped ball

With yarn C, make 6 dc in magic loop (see p.101). Pull tail to close.

Round 1: 2 dc in each dc to end. (12sts)
Round 2: *1 dc in next dc, 2 dc in next dc; rep from * to end. (18sts)
Round 3: *1 dc in each of next 2 dc, 2 dc in next dc; rep from * to end. (24sts)
Round 4: *1 dc in each of next 3 dc, 2 dc in next dc; rep from * to end. (30sts)
Round 5: *1 dc in each of next 4 dc, 2 dc in next dc; rep from * to end. (36sts)
Round 6: *1 dc in each of next 5 dc, 2 dc in next dc; rep from * to end. (42sts)
Round 7: *1 dc in each of next 6 dc, 2 dc in next dc; rep from * to end. (48sts)
Rounds 8–9: 1 dc in each dc to end, finish last dc with yarn A.

Round 10: With yarn A, work 1 dc in each dc to end, finish last dc with yarn B.
Rounds 11–12: With yarn B, work 1 dc in each dc to end, finish last dc of round 12 with yarn A.
Round 13: With yarn A, work 1 dc in each dc to end, finish last dc with yarn C.
Rounds 14–15: With yarn C, work 1 dc in each dc to end.
Round 16: *1 dc in each of next 6 dc, dc2tog; rep from * to end. (42sts)
Round 17: *1 dc in each of next 5 dc, dc2tog; rep from * to end. (36sts)
Round 18: *1 dc in each of next 4 dc, dc2tog; rep from * to end. (30sts)
Round 19: *1 dc in each of next 3 dc, dc2tog; rep from * to end. (24sts)
Round 20: *1 dc in each of next 2 dc, dc2tog; rep from * to end. (18sts)
Round 21: *1 dc in next dc, dc2tog; rep from * to end. (12sts)

Stuff very firmly.

Round 22: dc2tog to end. (6sts)

Fasten off, leaving a long tail. Use tail to close hole, weave in ends.

All-over striped ball

Follow above pattern, but change the yarn colour in each round, finishing the last st of prev round with new colour.

Tricoloured block ball

With yarn B, make 6 dc in magic loop (see p.101). Pull tail to close.

Round 1: 2 dc in each dc to end. (12sts)
Round 2: *1 dc in next dc, 2 dc in next dc; rep from * to end. (18sts)

Round 3: *1 dc in each of next 2 dc, 2 dc in next dc; rep from * to end. (24sts)
Round 4: *1 dc in each of next 3 dc, 2 dc in next dc; rep from * to end. (30sts)
Round 5: *1 dc in each of next 4 dc, 2 dc in next dc; rep from * to end. (36sts)
Round 6: *1 dc in each of next 5 dc, 2 dc in next dc; rep from * to end. (42sts)
Round 7: *1 dc in each of next 6 dc, 2 dc in next dc; rep from * to end, finish last st with yarn A. (48sts)
Rounds 8–15: With yarn A, work 1 dc in each dc to end, finish last st of round 15 with yarn C.
Round 16: With yarn C, *1 dc in each of next 6 dc, dc2tog; rep from * to end. (42sts)
Round 17: *1 dc in each of next 5 dc, dc2tog; rep from * to end. (36sts)
Round 18: *1 dc in each of next 4 dc, dc2tog; rep from * to end. (30sts)
Round 19: *1 dc in each of next 3 dc, dc2tog; rep from * to end. (24sts)
Round 20: *1 dc in each of next 2 dc, dc2tog; rep from * to end. (18sts)
Round 21: *1 dc in next dc, dc2tog; rep from * to end. (12sts)

Stuff very firmly.

Round 22: dc2tog to end. (6sts)

Fasten off, leaving a long tail. Use tail to close hole, weave in ends.

The starting and end points of the different coloured rounds form an off-set seam down the back of the ball.

Centre striped ball

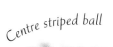

All-over striped ball

Tricoloured block ball

Kiddy slippers

These cuffed slippers are worked in the round, then crocheted flat before rejoining to create the slipper shape. The foot length is adjustable and, because the slipper is worked from the toe, it is easy to custom fit.

essential info ...

SIZE
To fit a child aged 2–3 years

YARN
A: Adriafil Stella Alpina Classic 50g x 1
B: Patons Diploma Gold DK 50g x 1

A   B

CROCHET HOOK
3.5mm hook
4.5mm hook

NOTIONS
Yarn needle

Slippers (Make 2)

With 4.5mm hook and yarn A, work 4 ch, join with a ss to form a ring.

Round 1: 6 dc into ring, do not join, cont working in a spiral using stitch marker to indicate the last st of each round (remove and replace after last dc of each round). Do not turn, cont to work in a spiral with RS facing.
Round 2: Work 2 dc in each dc. (12sts)
Round 3: *1 dc in next 2sts, 2 dc in next st, rep from * to end. (18sts)

Cont working in a spiral without increasing until toe measures 6cm (2½in). Turn. Remainder of the sole is worked flat.
Row 1: 1 ch, dc in second ch from hook, dc to last 6 dc, turn 12 dc.
Row 2: Dc to end.

Cont to work in dc until sole measures 12cm (5in) from round 1. Fasten off A.

With RS facing, sew heel seam. Turn slipper right way out and cont with RS facing.

With 4.5mm hook, rejoin A to centre of heel seam, 1 ch (does not count as a st), working in dc, work 1 row evenly around top piece of slipper, working 1 st into each row and each st across front of toe, ss into top of first dc to join.

Next row: Place markers in centre 2 toe stitches. 1 ch (does not count as st), dc to first marker, turn 1 ch, dc to second marker.

Cont working back and forth in dc, leaving the centre 2 stitches unworked.

Cont until cuff measures 2cm (¾in). For a longer cuff, work more rows here.

Final row: Dc to first marker, remove markers, dc2tog, dc to end. Fasten off.

With 3.5mm hook and B, join yarn to wrong side of top edge, work 2 rows of dc to finish.

Fasten off yarn, weave in all ends. Fold over cuff and sew in place.

tips ...

By using a slightly smaller crochet hook for the white cuff, the tension becomes tighter, too, so making the slippers even more secure.

By working in the round to start this pattern, the slippers have charming pointed toes.

To make the foot length longer, work additional rows 1 and 2.

The decorative stripes are made as part of the stitch pattern. Be sure to stitch in loose ends when switching colours.

Beanie hat

This cosy hat is made in the round starting at the top and increasing to the circumference of the head to fit the recipient. This hat has been made with two contrasting stripes near the brim, but it could easily be customized with additional stripes and colours.

essential info ...

SIZE
To fit an adult male

YARN
A: Wendy Aran 400g x 1
B: Debbie Bliss Cashmerino
 Aran 50g x 1

A   **B**

CROCHET HOOK
5mm hook

TENSION
11sts per 10cm (4in)

NOTIONS
Yarn needle

Special abbreviations

fphtr: front post half treble. Yrh and insert hook from front to back to front around the post of next st. Yrh and pull up a loop. Yrh and pull through all three loops on hook.

bphtr: back post half treble. Yrh and insert hook from back to front to back around the post of next st. Yrh and pull up a loop. Yrh and pull through all three loops on hook.

Beanie hat

With yarn A, work 4 ch, ss in first ch to form loop.

Round 1: 2 ch, 11 htr in loop, ss in top of first 2-ch to join. (12sts)
Round 2: 2 ch, 2 htr in next st. *1 htr in next st, 2 htr in next st; rep from * to end, ss in top of first 2-ch to join. (18sts)
Round 3: 2 ch, 1 htr in next st, 2 htr in next st. *1 htr in each of next 2sts, 2 htr in next st; rep from * to end, ss in top of first 2-ch to join. (24sts)
Round 4: 2 ch, 1 htr in each of next 2sts, 2 htr in next st. *1 htr in each of next 3sts, 2 htr in next st; rep from * to end, ss in top of first 2-ch to join. (30sts)
Round 5: 2 ch, 1 htr in each of next 3sts, 2 htr in next st. *1 htr in each of next 4sts, 2 htr in next st; rep from * to end, ss in top of first 2-ch to join. (36sts)
Round 6: 2 ch, 1 htr in each of next 4sts, 2 htr in next st. *1 htr in each of next 5sts, 2 htr in next st; rep from * to end, ss in top of first 2-ch to join. (42sts)
Round 7: 2 ch, 1 htr in each of next 5sts, 2 htr in next st. *1 htr in each of next 6sts, 2 htr in next st; rep from * to end, ss in top of first 2-ch to join. (48sts)
Round 8: 2 ch, 1 htr in each of next 6sts, 2 htr in next st. *1 htr in each of next 7sts, 2 htr in next st; rep from * to end, ss in top of first 2-ch to join. (54sts)
Round 9: 2 ch, 1 htr in each of next 7sts, 2 htr in next st. *1 htr in each of next 8sts, 2 htr in next st; rep from * to end, ss in top of first 2-ch to join. (60sts)
Increases can be stopped sooner or cont as set for a smaller or larger head size
Rounds 10–16: 2 ch, work 1 htr in each st to end, ss in top of first 2-ch to join.
Even rounds can be added or subtracted to adjust length of hat
Round 17: With yarn B, 2 ch, work 1 htr in each st to end, ss in top of first 2-ch to join.
Rounds 18–19: With yarn A, 2 ch, work 1 htr in each st to end, ss in top of first 2-ch to join.
Round 20: With yarn B, 2 ch, work 1 htr in each st to end, ss in top of first 2-ch to join.
Round 21: With yarn B, 2 ch, *fphtr in next st, bphtr in next st; rep from * to end, ss in top of first 2-ch to join.

Fasten off, weave in ends.

tips ...

Ensure that the starting hole is nearly closed after the first round. If not, pull out and start again with a shorter chain.

Round cushion

Concentric stripes in harmonious shades feature on this pretty cushion. Two flat circles are worked in the round and then sewn together at the edges. This is a quick project that works up easily, and is great for using up leftover lengths of yarn!

essential info ...

SIZE
35cm (14in) diameter

YARN
A: Debbie Bliss Cashmerino
    Aran 50g x 2
B: Debbie Bliss Cashmerino
    Aran 50g x 1
C: Debbie Bliss Cashmerino
    Aran 50g x 1
D: Debbie Bliss Cashmerino
    Aran 50g x 1

A B C D

CROCHET HOOK
5mm hook

NOTIONS
Round cushion pad,
    35cm (14in) diameter
Yarn needle

Round cushion

FRONT

With yarn A, work 4 ch, 12 tr in 4th ch from hook, ss in first st to join. (12sts)

Round 1: 3 ch, tr in same st. *2 tr in next st; rep from * around, ss in top of first 3-ch to join. (24sts)

Round 2: 3 ch, 2 tr in next st. *1 tr in next st, 2 tr in next st; rep from * around, ss in top of first 3-ch to join. (36sts)
Change to yarn B.

Round 3: 3 ch, 1 tr in next st, 2 tr in next st. *1 tr in each of next 2 sts, 2 tr in next st; rep from * around, ss in top of first 3-ch to join. (48sts)
Change to yarn C.

Round 4: 3 ch, 1 tr in each of next 2 sts, 2 tr in next st. *1 tr in each of next 3 sts, 2 tr in next st; rep from * around, ss in top of first 3-ch to join. (60sts)
Change to yarn D.

Round 5: 3 ch, 1 tr in each of next 3 sts, 2 tr in next st. *1 tr in each of next 4 sts, 2 tr in next st; rep from * around, ss in top of first 3-ch to join. (72sts)
Change to yarn A.

Round 6: 3 ch, 1 tr in each of next 4 sts, 2 tr in next st. *1 tr in each of next 5 sts, 2 tr in next st; rep from * around, ss in top of first 3-ch to join. (84sts)
Change to yarn B.

Cont in this way, working one additional single tr between increases per round and changing colour in this order every round, to 132sts, ending with yarn B.

The treble crochet stitch used for the cover forms a pretty, lacy pattern, showing a glimpse of the cushion underneath.

Work one further round in pattern in yarn B. (144sts)
Fasten off, weave in ends.

BACK
Work one more cushion side in the same way, but worked entirely in yarn A.

Finishing

Block pieces lightly (see p.132). Sew together two pieces around circumference, trapping cushion pad inside.

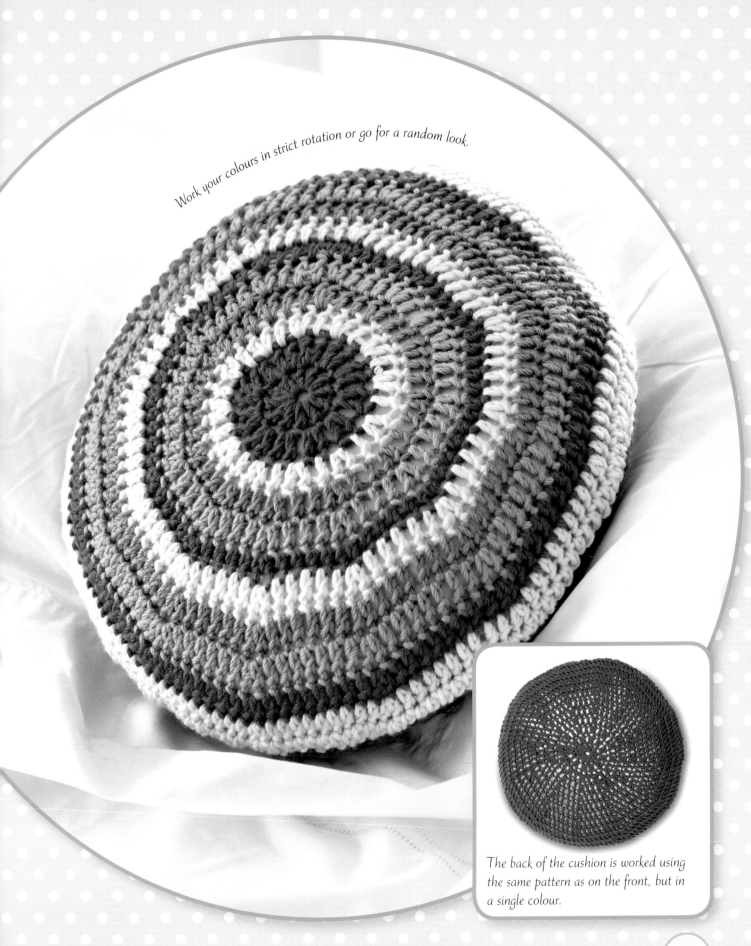

Work your colours in strict rotation or go for a random look.

The back of the cushion is worked using the same pattern as on the front, but in a single colour.

Crocheting medallions

The principle for starting any medallion shape and working it in rounds is the same as for the simple circle, and many simple crochet flowers are also worked using these techniques (see pp.124–125). If you find it awkward to fit all the stitches of the first round into a tiny foundation ring (see pp.100–101), try the simple loop ring below. Two other useful tips are the techniques for starting new colours and for joining motifs together (see opposite).

Making a simple loop ring

1 **Making the simple** loop ring is a quick way to start working a flat shape in the round, and it allows you to make the centre hole as tight or as open as desired. Start as if you are making a slip knot (see p.24), by forming a circle of yarn and drawing the yarn through the centre of it.

2 **Leave the circle** of yarn open. Then, to start a round of double crochet stitches, make 1 chain.

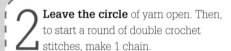

3 **Work the first** round of double crochet stitches, working them into the ring and over the yarn tail as shown by the large arrow.

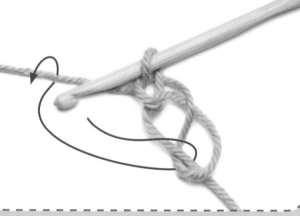

4 **When all the** required stitches are worked into the ring, pull the yarn tail to close the ring. Then continue as explained in the pattern instructions.

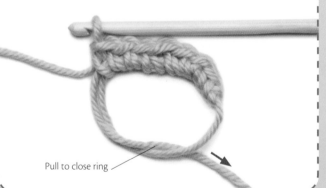

Pull to close ring

Joining on a new colour

When starting a new colour at the beginning of a medallion round, you can either change to the new colour with the last yrh of the previous round or fasten off the old colour and join on a new colour with a slip stitch.

New colour

Old colour

Slip knot

1 **Joining on the** new colour with a slip stitch makes a firm attachment. Make a slip knot with the new colour and remove it from the hook. Then insert the hook at the specified position and draw the slip knot through.

2 **Start the new** round with the specified number of chains, drawing the first chain through the slip knot. Work the stitches of the round over both yarn tails (the new colour and the old colour) so that there aren't so many ends to darn in later. Alternatively, to reduce bulk, start the new colour in a different place and weave in one tail at a time.

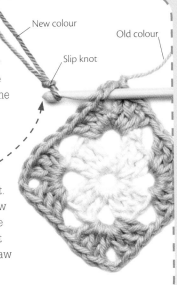

Work stitches over yarn tails

Joining medallions

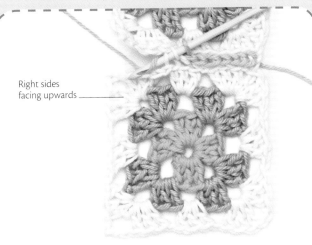

Right sides facing upwards

Double-crochet seam: A double crochet seam is also quick to work. It forms a ridge, which can either be a feature on the right side, or hidden on the wrong side of the work. Place the two medallions together, either wrong side to wrong side (ridge on right side), or right side to right side (ridge on wrong side). Then work each double crochet through only 1 loop of the top of a stitch on each medallion (the loop closest to you on the top medallion and the loop farthest from you on the bottom medallion).

Right sides together

Flat slip-stitch seam: Working seams with crochet stitches are the quickest way to join medallions. For a slip-stitch seam, lay the two medallions side by side. Work each slip stitch through only 1 loop (the back loop) of the top of a stitch on each medallion. (Use a hook one size smaller than the hook used for the medallions, but work the stitches very loosely.)

Medallion and flower patterns

Making crochet medallions and flowers is a great way to use up yarn scraps, and this was probably the reason they became so popular. You can stitch medallions together to form small items like bags or cushion covers, or to form larger items like throws, baby blankets, and scarves. Crochet flowers make great individual brooches, which, in turn, are perfect gifts. Just sew brooch pins to the back and maybe a button or an artificial pearl to the flower centre (see pp.126–127). Crochet flowers and leaves can also be used to decorate crocheted hats, the ends of scarves, glove cuffs, or bags.

Simple medallion shapes

Traditional afghan square

This square is worked in 4 colours (A, B, C, D), a different colour for each round.

Using A, make 4 ch and join with a ss to first ch to form a ring.

Round 1 (RS): Using A, 5 ch (counts as 1 tr and a 2-ch sp), [3 tr in ring, 2 ch (these 2-ch form a corner sp)] 3 times, 2 tr in ring, join with a ss to 3rd of 5-ch. Fasten off A.

Round 2: Using B, join with a ss to a 2-ch corner sp, 5 ch, 3 tr in same corner sp, *1 ch, [3 tr, 2 ch, 3 tr] in next 2-ch corner sp; rep from * twice more, 1 ch, 2 tr in same corner sp as 5-ch at beg of round, join with a ss to 3rd of 5-ch. Fasten off B.

Round 3: Using C, join to a 2-ch corner sp, 5 ch, 3 tr in same corner sp, *1 ch, 3 tr in next 1-ch sp, 1 ch, [3 tr, 2 ch, 3 tr] in next 2-ch corner sp; rep from * twice more, 1 ch, 3 tr in next 1-ch sp, 1 ch, 2 tr in same sp as 5-ch at beg of round, join with a ss to 3rd of 5-ch. Fasten off C.

Round 4: Using D, join to a 2-ch corner sp, 5 ch, 3 tr in same corner sp, *[1 ch, 3 tr in next 1-ch sp] twice, 1 ch, [3 tr, 2 ch, 3 tr] in next 2-ch corner sp; rep from * twice more, [1 ch, 3 tr in next 1-ch sp] twice, 1 ch, 2 tr in same sp as 5-ch at beg of round, join with a ss to 3rd of 5-ch. **Fasten off.**

Special notes
- Join on new colours as explained on p.121.
- Do not turn the medallions at the end of the rounds, but work with the right side always facing.
- If you are a beginner, stick to less hairy yarns when making your first medallions as it is easier to learn the technique with a smooth standard lightweight or medium-weight wool yarn.

Plain square

This square is worked in 3 colours (A, B, C).

Using A, make 4 ch and join with a ss to first ch to form a ring.

Round 1 (RS): 5 ch (counts as 1 tr and a 2-ch sp), [3 tr in ring, 2 ch] 3 times, 2 tr in ring, join with a ss to 3rd of 5-ch.

Round 2: 1 ss in next ch, 7 (counts as 1 tr and a 4-ch sp), 2 tr in same 2-ch corner sp, *1 tr in each of next 3 tr, [2 tr, 4 ch, 2 tr] in next 2-ch corner sp; rep from * twice more, 1 tr in each of next 3 sts (working last of these tr in top of turning ch at beg of previous round), 1 tr in same sp as 7-ch at beg of round, join with a ss to 3rd of 7-ch. Fasten off A.

Round 3: Using B, join to a 4-ch corner sp, 7 ch, 2 tr in same corner sp, *1 tr in each of tr along this side of square, [2 tr, 4 ch, 2 tr] in next 4-ch corner sp; rep from * twice more, 1 tr in each of tr along this side of square (working last of these tr in top of turning ch at beg of previous round), 1 tr in same sp as 7-ch at beg of round, join with a ss to 3rd of 7-ch. Fasten off B.

Round 4: Using C, rep round 3.

Fasten off.

Simple hexagon

Note: cluster (cl) = [yrh and insert hook in sp, yrh and draw a loop through, yrh and draw through first 2 loops on hook] 3 times all in same sp (4 loops now on hook), yrh and draw through all 4 loops on hook.

This hexagon is worked in 3 colours (A, B, C).

Using A, make 6 ch and join with a ss to first ch to form a ring.

Round 1 (RS): 3 ch, tr2tog (counts as first cl), [3 ch, 1 cl in ring] 5 times, 1 ch, join with 1 htr in top of first cl.

Round 2: 3 ch, tr2tog in sp formed by 1-htr, *3 ch, [1 cl, 3 ch, 1 cl] in next 3-ch sp; rep from * 4 times more, 3 ch, 1 cl in next 1-ch sp, 1 ch, join with 1 htr in top of first cl changing to B with last yrh of htr. Cut off A.

Round 3: Using B, 3 ch, tr2tog in sp formed by 1-htr, *3 ch, [1 cl, 3 ch, 1 cl] in next 3-ch sp, 3 ch, 1 cl in next 3-ch sp; rep from * 4 times more, 3 ch, [1 cl, 3 ch, 1 cl] in next 3-ch sp, 1 ch, join with 1 htr in top of first cl changing to C with last yrh of htr. Fasten off B.

Round 4: Using C, 3 ch, 1 tr in sp formed by 1-htr, *3 tr in next 3-ch sp, [3 tr, 2 ch, 3 tr] in next 3-ch sp, 3 tr in next 3-ch sp; rep from * 4 times more, 3 tr in next 3-ch sp, [3 tr, 2 ch, 3 tr] in next 3-ch sp, 1 tr in next 1-ch sp, join with a ss to 3rd of 3-ch at beg of round.

Fasten off.

Simple flower shapes

Button flower

Note: cluster = [yrh twice and insert hook in sp, yrh and draw a loop through, (yrh and draw through first 2 loops on hook) twice] 4 times all in same sp (5 loops now on hook), yrh and draw through all 5 loops now on hook.

This flower is worked in 2 colours (A, B).

Using A, make 4 ch and join with a ss to first ch to form a ring.

Round 1 (RS): 4 ch (counts as first dtr), 20 dtr in ring, join with a ss to 4th of 4-ch. Fasten off A.

Round 2: Using B, join with a ss to same place as last ss, 1 ch (does NOT count as a st), 1 dc in same place as last ss, [5 ch, miss next 2 dtr, 1 dc in next dtr] 6 times, 5 ch, join with a ss to first dc of round.

Round 3: *Work [1 ss, 4 ch, 1 cluster, 4 ch, 1 ss] all in next 5-ch loop; rep from * 6 times more, join with a ss to last dc in round 2.

Fasten off. Sew a small button onto the centre of the flower.

Short loop flower

This flower is worked in 2 colours (A, B).

Using A, make 4 ch and join with a ss to first ch to form a ring.

Round 1 (RS): 1 ch (does NOT count as a st), 8 dc in ring, join with a ss to first dc of round.

Round 2: 1 ch (does NOT count as a st), 2 dc in same place as ss, *2 dc in next dc; rep from * to end, join with a ss to first dc of round. 16 dc. Fasten off A.

Round 3: Using B, join with a ss to a dc, 1 ch, work [1 dc, 9 ch, 1 dc] all in same place as last ss, 1 dc in next dc, *work [1 dc, 9 ch, 1 dc] all in next dc, 1 dc in next dc; rep from * 6 times more, join with a ss to first dc of round.

Fasten off.

Long loop flower

This flower is worked in 3 colours (A, B, C).

Using A, make 4 ch and join with a ss to first ch to form a ring.

Round 1 (RS): 1 ch (does NOT count as a st), 8 dc in ring, join with a ss to first dc of round. Fasten off A.

Round 2: Using B, join with a ss to a dc, 1 ch (does NOT count as a st), 2 dc in same place as last ss, *2 dc in next dc; rep from * to end, join with a ss to first dc of round. 16 dc. Fasten off B.

Round 3: Using C, join with a ss to a dc, 1 ch, work [1 dc, 17 ch, 1 dc] all in same place as last ss, *work [1 dc, 17 ch, 1 dc] all in next dc; rep from * 14 times more, join with a ss to first dc of round.

Fasten off.

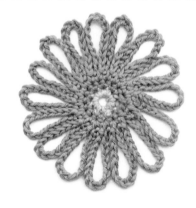

Pentagon flower

This flower is worked in 2 colours (A, B).

Using A, make 5 ch and join with a ss to first ch to form a ring.

Round 1 (RS): 3 ch (counts as first tr), 4 tr in ring, [1 ch, 5 tr in ring] 4 times, 1 ch, join with a ss to top of 3-ch at beg of round. Fasten off A.

Round 2: Using B, join with a ss to a centre tr of a 5-tr group, 1 ch, 1 dc in same place as last ss, [7 dtr in next 1-ch sp, 1 dc in centre tr of next 5-tr group] 4 times, 7 dtr in next 1-ch sp, join with a ss to first dc of round. **Fasten off.**

Square petal flower

This flower is worked in 3 colours (A, B, C).

Using A, make 4 ch and join with a ss to first ch to form a ring.

Round 1 (RS): 3 ch (counts as first tr), 11 tr in ring, join with a ss to top of 3-ch at beg of round. Fasten off A.

Round 2: Using B, join with a ss same place as last ss, 1 ch (does NOT count as a st), 2 dc in same place as last ss, 2 dc in each tr to end, join with a ss to first dc of round. 24 dc. Fasten off B.

Round 3: Using C, join with a ss to a dc, *4 ch, 1 dtr in next dc, 2 dtr in next dc, 1 dtr in next dc, 4 ch, 1 ss in next dc; rep from * 5 times more working last ss in same place as first ss of round.

Fasten off.

Simple leaf

Note: The leaf is worked in one row, around both sides of the foundation chain.

To begin leaf and stem, make 23 ch.

Row 1 (RS): Working into only one loop of each foundation chain, work 1 dc in 2nd ch from hook, 1 dc in each of next 10 ch (this completes the stem), 1 htr in next ch, 1 tr in each of next 2 ch, 1 dtr in each of next 4 ch, 1 tr in each of next 2 ch, 1 htr in next ch, 1 dc in next ch (this is the last ch), 3 ch, then continue working around other side of foundation ch (working into other loop of each ch) as follows – 1 dc in first ch, 1 htr in next ch, 1 tr in each of next 2 ch, 1 dtr in each of next 4 ch, 1 tr in each of next 2 ch, 1 htr in next ch, 1 ss in next ch.
Fasten off, then press stem flat.

A bunch of daisies

These fancy flowers are a perfect way to decorate your clothes and accessories. Create all kinds of variations; from the number of petals to the combination of colours.

essential info ...

SIZE
5cm–7.5cm (2in–3in) diameter

YARN
Scraps of cotton yarn in various colours

CROCHET HOOK
4.5mm hook

NOTIONS
Yarn needle

4-petalled flowers

Work 6 ch, ss into the first ch to join the ring.

Round 1: Make 1 ch, work 12 dc into the ring, ss into first ch to join together.
Round 2: Make 6 ch, *miss 2 dc; dc into next st, 6 ch; rep from* to the end of the round, ss into bottom of first 6 ch.
Round 3: *work (1 dc, 1 htr, 5 tr, 1 htr, 1 dc) into next 6 ch space, ss into dc, rep from * to the end of the round.

Fasten off, weave in all ends.

5- and 6-petalled flowers

To make more petals, simply add more double crochet stitches into the ring.

5 petals: Make a ring as above.
Round 1: Work 15 dc into the ring, ss into first ch to join the ring.
Rounds 2–3: Work as for 4 petals, above.

6 petals: Make a ring as above.
Round 1: Work 18 dc into the ring, ss into first ch to join the ring.
Rounds 2–3: Work as for 4 petals, above.

Round 1

Rounds 1 and 2

Rounds 1, 2, and 3

tips ...

To make a brooch, layer up the flowers and sew them together. Attach a button to the centre front, then sew a safety pin to the back of the flower. Stitch over and over the back of the pin to secure it.

Once you have got the hang of making a four-petalled daisy, try adding more petals by adapting the pattern. Each daisy is made up in three stages and each of these also makes a pretty motif by itself.

Top off your hairbands and hats with flowers too. Here the flowers are stitched together, then sewn to the band.

Baby's blanket

This adorable baby blanket is made as a large Afghan (or Granny) square with a centre of mini squares and finished with a shell edging. Each new colour is joined directly to the previous square or round, so no seaming is required – just weave in the ends to finish.

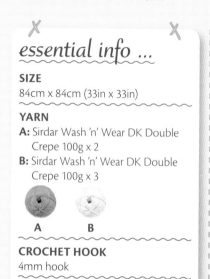

essential info ...

SIZE
84cm x 84cm (33in x 33in)

YARN
A: Sirdar Wash 'n' Wear DK Double Crepe 100g x 2
B: Sirdar Wash 'n' Wear DK Double Crepe 100g x 3

A   B

CROCHET HOOK
4mm hook

NOTIONS
Yarn needle

Mini squares

With yarn A, work 4 ch, ss to first ch to form loop.

Round 1: 3 ch, 2 tr in loop. *2 ch, 3 tr in loop; rep from * twice more, 2 ch, ss in top of beg 3-ch to join. Fasten off yarn A.

For next mini square, use the join-as-you-go-method.

With yarn B, work 4 ch, ss to first ch to form loop.
Round 1: 3 ch, 2 tr in loop. *dc in any 2-ch corner sp of starting mini square, 3 tr in loop of current square; rep from * once more. 2 ch, 3 tr in loop, 2 ch, ss in top of beg 3-ch to join. Fasten off yarn B.

Cont making and joining the mini squares as you go, alternating colours, until centre large square is desired size. Sample blanket uses 6 x 6 mini squares.

Granny square rounds

Join yarn A in next ch sp after any corner.

Round 1: 3 ch, 2 tr into same space. *1 ch, 3 tr into next ch sp; rep from * to corner, work (3 tr, 2 ch, 3 tr) in corner space. Rep around piece. Fasten off yarn A.
Rounds 2–3: Attach yarn B and rep round 1. At the end of round 2, ss in top of beg 3-ch, ss in each st to next ch sp from prev round, then begin as round 1. Fasten off yarn B.
Round 4: Attach yarn A and rep round 1.

Rep rounds 1–3 to form pattern, one round of yarn A and two rounds of yarn B.

Cont with Granny rounds until blanket is desired size. Sample blanket uses 24 rounds, ending on a round 3.

Edging

Round 1: Attach yarn B in any st. Dc in each st and ch around blanket, working 3 dc in each corner sp. Ss in first dc to join. Fasten off yarn B.
Round 2: Attach yarn A. 2 ch, *5 tr in next dc, dc into next dc. Rep from * around blanket.

Fasten off, weave in all ends.

A central block of mini squares is surrounded by rounds of traditional Afghan (or Granny) square stitch.

The outermost stripe in this design is uses shell edging. It finishes the blanket without breaking up the pattern of stripes.

Patchwork blanket

This beautiful blanket is made up of individual squares – a variation of the plain square shown on p.123 – which are then joined together and finished with a border. The squares can be crocheted all at once or over time.

essential info ...

SIZE
110cm x 94cm (43in x 37in)

YARN
A: Stylecraft Special DK 100g x 3
B: Stylecraft Special DK 100g x 2
B: Stylecraft Special DK 100g x 2

A   B   C

CROCHET HOOK
4mm hook

NOTIONS
Yarn needle

Square

With yarn A, work 4 ch, ss in first ch to form loop.

Round 1: 3 ch, 2 tr in loop, *2 ch, 3 tr in loop, rep from * twice more, 2 ch, ss in top of beg 3-ch to join. Fasten off yarn A.

Round 2: Join yarn B in any centre tr from 3-tr set from prev round. 3 ch, *1 tr in each tr to corner sp. Work (2 tr, 4 ch, 2 tr) in next 2-ch corner sp; rep from * to end, work 1 tr in each rem tr, ss in top of beg 3-ch to join. (7 tr per side of square)

Round 3: 3 ch, *1 tr in each tr to corner. Work (2 tr, 4 ch, 2 tr) in 4-ch corner sp. Rep from * to end, work 1 tr in each rem tr, ss in top of beg 3-ch to join. (11 tr per side of square) Fasten off yarn B.

Round 4: Join yarn A in any tr st. Rep round 3 with yarn A. (15 tr per side of square) Fasten off yarn A.

Make 27 more squares using yarn B in rounds 2 and 3 (28 B squares total), and 28 squares using yarn C in rounds 2 and 3.

JOIN SQUARES

Lay two squares right sides facing. Work dc join in back loops only of each st. Join squares into strips of 8 squares. Lay two strips of 8 right sides facing. Work dc join in back loops only of each st. Cont until all squares are joined. Sample blanket uses 7 x 8 squares.

Edging

Round 1: Join yarn A in any tr. 3 ch, *1 tr in each tr to corner sp. Work (2 tr, 4 ch, 2 tr) into each 4-ch corner sp. Rep from * around entire blanket, work 1 tr in each rem tr, ss in top of beg 3-ch to join.

Round 2: Rep round 1.

Fasten off, weave in all ends.

Alternate block colours as shown, or add others to create your own colour combinations.

The size of the blanket can easily be varied by increasing or decreasing the number of squares in each row or column.

The squares of the blanket are joined by working through only the back loops of each stitch. This helps the blanket lie flat.

Blocking and seams

Always sew the seams on a garment or accessory using a blunt-ended needle and a matching yarn (a contrasting yarn is used here just to show the seam techniques more clearly); and work them in the order given in the crochet pattern. But before sewing any seams, block your crochet pieces carefully. Press the finished seams very lightly with a cool iron on the wrong side after completion.

Wet blocking

If your yarn will allow it, wet blocking is the best way to even out crochet. Wet the pieces in a sink full of lukewarm water. Then squeeze out the water and roll the crochet in a towel to remove excess dampness. Smooth the crochet into shape right-side down on layers of dry towels covered with a sheet, pinning at intervals. Add as many pins as is necessary to refine the shape. Do not move the crochet until it is completely dry.

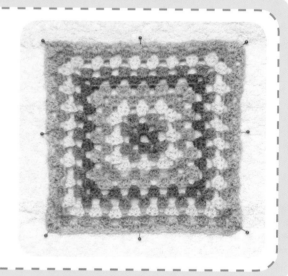

Steam blocking

For a speedier process you may prefer steam blocking (if your yarn label allows it). First, pin the crochet right-side down into the correct shape. Then steam the crochet gently using a clean damp cloth, but barely touching the cloth with the iron. Never rest the weight of an iron on your crochet or it will flatten the texture. Leave the steamed piece to dry completely before unpinning it.

Backstitch seam

Backstitch produces durable seams and is frequently recommended in crochet patterns for garments and accessories.

1 Align the crochet pieces with right sides together and secure the yarn with two or three overcast stitches in the same place. Then, inserting the needle close to the edge, work the seam taking one stitch forwards and one stitch back.

Blunt-ended yarn needle

2 On the backwards stitch, be sure to insert the needle through the same place as the end of the last stitch. At the end of the seam, secure the yarn in the same way as at the beginning of the seam.

Overcast stitch seam *(also called whip stitch)*

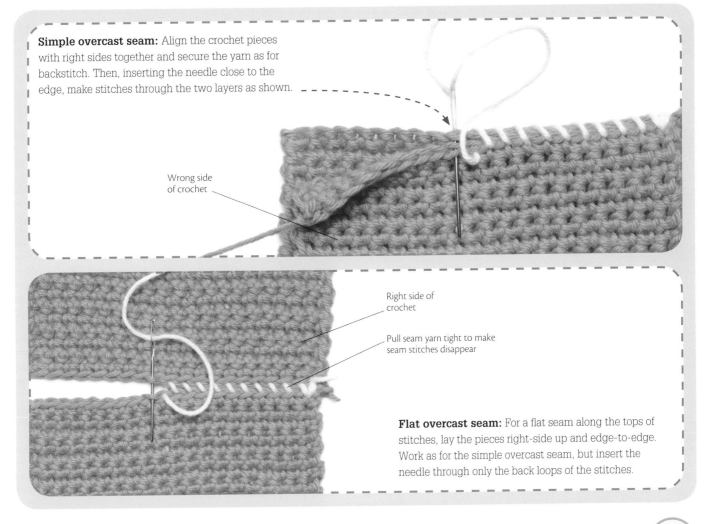

Simple overcast seam: Align the crochet pieces with right sides together and secure the yarn as for backstitch. Then, inserting the needle close to the edge, make stitches through the two layers as shown.

Wrong side of crochet

Right side of crochet

Pull seam yarn tight to make seam stitches disappear

Flat overcast seam: For a flat seam along the tops of stitches, lay the pieces right-side up and edge-to-edge. Work as for the simple overcast seam, but insert the needle through only the back loops of the stitches.

Edge-to-edge seam (also called mattress stitch)

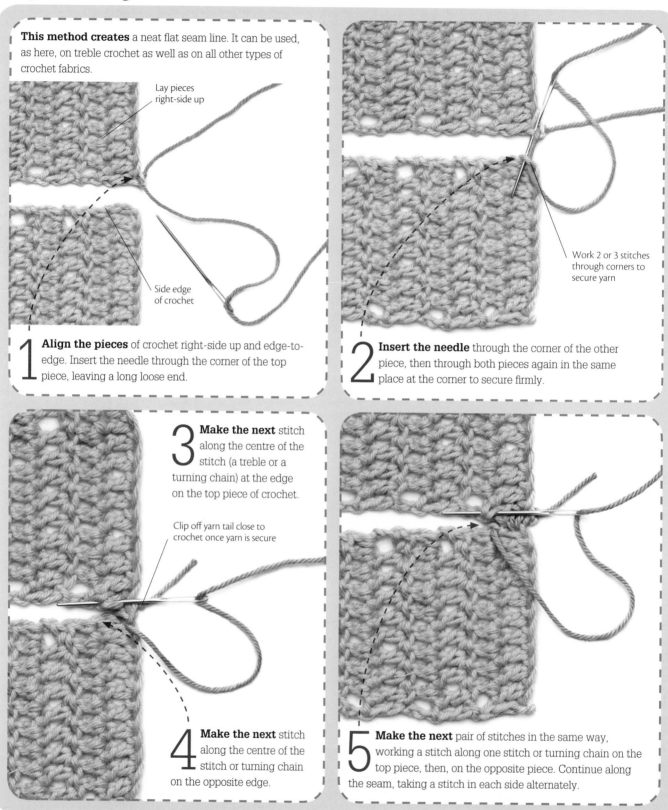

This method creates a neat flat seam line. It can be used, as here, on treble crochet as well as on all other types of crochet fabrics.

Lay pieces right-side up

Side edge of crochet

1 **Align the pieces** of crochet right-side up and edge-to-edge. Insert the needle through the corner of the top piece, leaving a long loose end.

Work 2 or 3 stitches through corners to secure yarn

2 **Insert the needle** through the corner of the other piece, then through both pieces again in the same place at the corner to secure firmly.

3 **Make the next** stitch along the centre of the stitch (a treble or a turning chain) at the edge on the top piece of crochet.

Clip off yarn tail close to crochet once yarn is secure

4 **Make the next** stitch along the centre of the stitch or turning chain on the opposite edge.

5 **Make the next** pair of stitches in the same way, working a stitch along one stitch or turning chain on the top piece, then, on the opposite piece. Continue along the seam, taking a stitch in each side alternately.

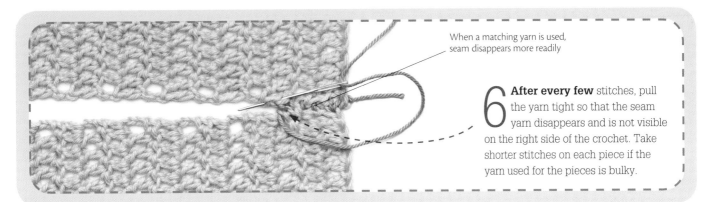

When a matching yarn is used, seam disappears more readily

6 **After every few** stitches, pull the yarn tight so that the seam yarn disappears and is not visible on the right side of the crochet. Take shorter stitches on each piece if the yarn used for the pieces is bulky.

Slip stitch seam

1 **Instead of using** a yarn needle to join your seam, you can use a crochet hook to work a quicker seam. Although seams can be worked with double crochet, slip stitch seams are less bulky. Start by placing a slip knot on the hook.

Start with a slip knot on the hook

Seam yarn

2 **Align the two** layers of crochet with the right sides together.

3 **Then with the** slip knot on the hook, insert the hook through the two layers at the starting end of the seam, wrap the yarn around the hook, and draw a loop through the two layers and the loop on the hook.

4 **Continue in this** way and fasten off at the end. When working the seam along the tops of stitches (as here), insert the hook through only the back loops of the stitches. Along row-end edges, work through the layers one stitch in from the edge.

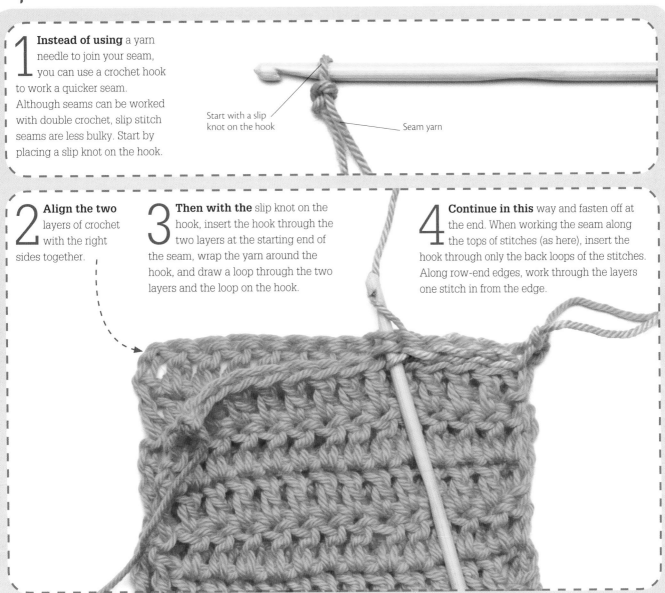

Fastenings and finishes

Many types of fastenings can be used on crocheted items. While some of them are purely functional, securing closings on garments and accessories, others can serve as a decorative finish as well as being practical. Always attach fastenings with care.

Sewing on a 2-hole button

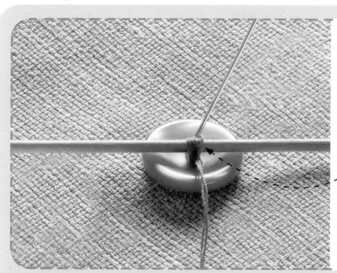

1 **A cocktail stick** will help you to sew on this type of button. Position the button on the fabric. Start with double thread in the needle. Take a stitch, and loop back through it to form a double stitch to secure the thread.

2 **Place a cocktail stick** on top of the button. Stitch up and down through the holes, going over the stick.

3 **Remove the cocktail stick.** Wrap the thread around the thread loops under the button to make a shank.

4 **Take the thread** through to the back of the fabric. Take short, closely-spaced stitches (known as buttonhole stitches) over the loop of threads on the back of the work.

Sewing on a 4-hole button

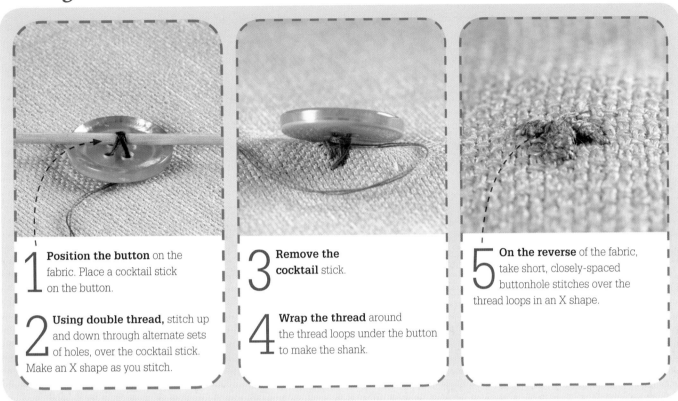

1 **Position the button** on the fabric. Place a cocktail stick on the button.

2 **Using double thread,** stitch up and down through alternate sets of holes, over the cocktail stick. Make an X shape as you stitch.

3 **Remove the cocktail** stick.

4 **Wrap the thread** around the thread loops under the button to make the shank.

5 **On the reverse** of the fabric, take short, closely-spaced buttonhole stitches over the thread loops in an X shape.

Sewing on a shanked button

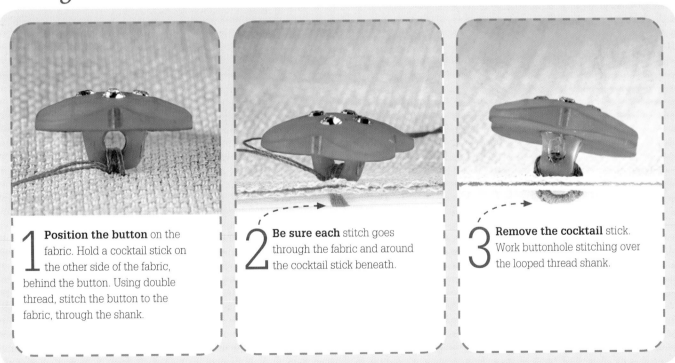

1 **Position the button** on the fabric. Hold a cocktail stick on the other side of the fabric, behind the button. Using double thread, stitch the button to the fabric, through the shank.

2 **Be sure each** stitch goes through the fabric and around the cocktail stick beneath.

3 **Remove the cocktail** stick. Work buttonhole stitching over the looped thread shank.

Making a fringe

1 **Cut two lengths** of yarn, twice the length of the finished fringe, plus at least 2.5cm (1in) extra for the knots.

2 **Align the two** strands and fold them in half. With the wrong side of the fabric facing, insert a crochet hook from front to back, 5mm (¼in) from the edge. Draw the loop through.

Wrong side

3 **Using the crochet** hook, pull the ends of the strands through the loop on the hook. Tighten the loop to secure the fringe

4 **Measure your fringe** after making this first fringe knot to ensure that it is long enough, and adjust the length of the strands if necessary.

5 **Add fringe knots** along the edge of the fabric, spacing them evenly apart. For a plumper fringe, use more than two strands at a time. If you have trouble pulling the fringe through the fabric, experiment using a smaller or larger hook

6 **After completing the** fringe, trim it slightly to straighten the ends if necessary.

Right side

Yarn embellishments for crochet are easy to make, but be sure to take your time so that they look absolutely perfect. Fringe is often used to edge throws and scarves; tassels are ideal for the corners of a cushion cover or the top of a hat.

Making a tassel

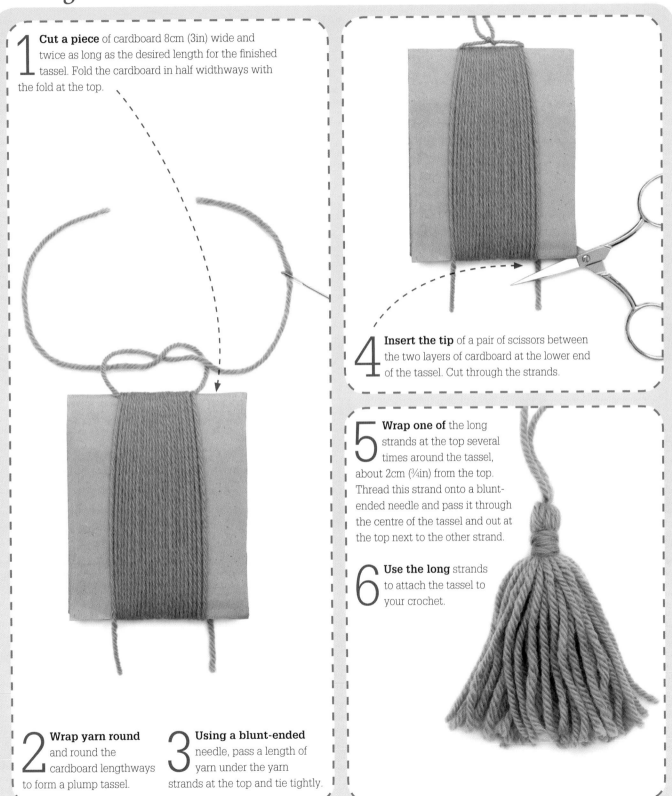

1 **Cut a piece** of cardboard 8cm (3in) wide and twice as long as the desired length for the finished tassel. Fold the cardboard in half widthways with the fold at the top.

2 **Wrap yarn round** and round the cardboard lengthways to form a plump tassel.

3 **Using a blunt-ended** needle, pass a length of yarn under the yarn strands at the top and tie tightly.

4 **Insert the tip** of a pair of scissors between the two layers of cardboard at the lower end of the tassel. Cut through the strands.

5 **Wrap one of** the long strands at the top several times around the tassel, about 2cm (¾in) from the top. Thread this strand onto a blunt-ended needle and pass it through the centre of the tassel and out at the top next to the other strand.

6 **Use the long** strands to attach the tassel to your crochet.

Glossary

Acrylic
Man-made fibres spun into yarn resembling wool.

Aran yarn
Also called medium, 12-ply, worsted, or Afghan. A medium yarn suitable for jumpers, menswear, blankets, hats, scarves, and mittens.

Ballband
The wrapper around a ball of yarn, which usually details fibre content, weight, length, hook size, tension, and cleaning instructions.

Ball-winder
A device for winding hanks of yarn into balls; also used to wind two or more strands together to make a double-stranded yarn. Often used in conjunction with a swift.

Blocking
Manipulating a finished piece into the correct shape by wetting and pinning it out, or pinning it out and steam pressing it.

Bulky or chunky yarn
Also called 14-ply, craft, or rug (yarn symbol 5). A chunky yarn suitable for rugs, jackets, blankets, hats, legwarmers, and winter accessories.

Cashmere
From Kashmir goats; the most luxurious of all wools.

Chain loop, chain space
A length of chain stitches worked between basic stitches to create a space in the fabric.

Colourwork
Any method of incorporating colour into your crochet. This includes stripes, jacquard, and intarsia.

Decrease
Removing a stitch or stitches in order to reduce the number of working stitches and shape the fabric.

Double-knit yarn (DK)
A medium-weight yarn. Also called DK, 5–6-ply, or light worsted (yarn symbol 3). A light yarn suitable for jumpers, lightweight scarves, blankets, and toys.

Fibres
Yarn is made up of fibres, such as the hair from an animal, man-made (synthetic) fibres, or fibres derived from a plant. The fibres are processed and spun into a yarn.

Filet crochet
A form of openwork crochet created by working a combination of squares or rectangles of open mesh and solid blocks.

Fine yarn
Also called 4-ply, sport, or baby (yarn symbol 2). A fine yarn is suitable for lightweight jumpers, babywear, socks, and accessories.

Foundation chain
A length of chain stitches that forms the base of the piece of crochet.

Hank
A twisted ring of yarn, which needs to be wound into one or more balls before it can be used.

Hook and eye fastening
Two-part metal fastening used to fasten overlapping edges of fabric where a neat join is required. Available in a wide variety of styles.

Increase
Adding a stitch or stitches to increase the number of working stitches and shape the fabric.

Intarsia
A term used to refer to a technique in which a colour appears only in a section of a row. More than two colours may be used in a row. A separate ball or length of yarn is used for each area of colour and carried vertically up to the next row when it is needed again.

Jacquard crochet
A type of colourwork crochet worked in double crochet stitch, with no more than two colours in each row. The colour not in use is carried across the top of the row below and covered with the stitches of the other colour so it is hidden from view.

Lace yarn
Also called 2-ply or fingering (yarn symbol 0). A very fine yarn for crocheting lace.

Lanolin
An oily substance contained in sheeps' wool.

Medallion
A flat shape worked from the centre outwards.

Mercerized cotton
Cotton thread, fabric, or yarn that has been treated in order to strengthen it and add a sheen. The yarn is a good choice for items that need to be strong and hold a shape, such as a bag.

Mohair
Fluffy wool yarn spun from the hair of Angora goats.

Notion
An item of haberdashery, other than fabric, needed to complete a project, such as a button, zip, or elastic.

Nylon
Hard-wearing, man-made fabric.

Openwork crochet
A lacelike effect created by working chain spaces and/or loops between the basic stitches.

Plied yarn
A yarn made from more than one strand of spun fibre, so 4-ply is four strands plied together. Most yarns are plied, as plying prevents the yarn from twisting and the resulting fabric from slanting diagonally.

Right side
The front of a piece of fabric, the side that will normally be in view when the piece is made up.

Round
A row worked in a circle, with the last stitch of the row being joined to the first to complete the foundation circle.

Seam
The join formed when two pieces of fabric are sewn together.

Silk
Threads spun by the silkworm and used to create cool, luxurious fabrics.

Slip knot
A knot that you form when you place the first loop on the hook.

Slip stitch
The shortest of all the crochet stitches. Although slip stitches can be worked in rows, the resulting fabric is very dense and suitable only for bag handles. Slip stitches are frequently used in crochet projects, for example to join on new yarn, to work invisibly along the top of a row to move to a new position, and to join rounds in circular crochet.

Skein
Yarn wound into a long oblong shape, which is ready to crochet.

Snaps
Also known as press studs, these fasteners are used as lightweight hidden fasteners.

Super bulky or super chunky yarn
Also called 16-ply (and upwards), bulky, or roving (yarn symbol 6). A chunky yarn suitable for heavy blankets, rugs, and thick scarves.

Superfine yarn
Also called 3-ply, fingering, or baby (yarn symbol 1). A very fine yarn suitable for fine-knit socks, shawls, and babywear.

Tape measure
Flexible form of ruler made from plastic or fabric.

Tape yarn
A wide, flat, or tubular yarn, flattened when wound into a ball. Can be crocheted to produce a nubbly or smooth result.

Tension
The number of stitches and rows over a given area, usually 10cm (4in) square. Also, the relative tightness used by the crocheter.

Turning chain
A length of chain stitches worked at the start of a row to bring the hook up to the necessary height to work the first stitch of that row.

Velcro™
Two-part fabric fastening consisting of two layers, a "hook" side and a "loop" side; when pressed together the two pieces cling together.

Weaving in ends
The process of completing a piece of crochet by weaving yarn ends into the crochet to disguise them.

Wool
A natural animal fibre, available in a range of weights, weaves, and textures. It is warm, comfortable to wear, and crease-resistant.

Wrong side
The reverse of a piece of fabric, the side that will normally be hidden from view when the piece is made up.

Yarn
Fibres that have been spun into a long strand. Yarns may be made of natural fibres, man-made fibres, a blend of the two, or even non-standard materials.

Yarn bobbins
Small plastic shapes for holding yarn when doing intarsia work, where there are many yarns in different colours.

Zip
Fastening widely used on garments consisting of two strips of fabric tape, carrying specially shaped metal or plastic teeth that lock together by means of a pull or slider. Zips are available in different colours and weights.

Index

Acknowledgements

Dorling Kindersley would like to thank:

Jane Bull, for her projects: Crowls (p.38), Bag of stripes (p.72), and A bunch of daisies (p.126) (Photography: Andy Crawford).

Sally Harding, author of the tools, materials and techniques sections and creator of the Toy Dog (p.106) (Photography: Peter Anderson). Sally is a needlecraft technician, author, designer, and editor. She was the Technical Knitting Editor for *Vogue Knitting* from 1982, and has for many years edited needlecraft books by acclaimed textile designer Kaffe Fassett. Her books include *Crochet Style* (1987), *Fast Knits Fat Needles* (2005), and *Quick Crochet Huge Hooks* (2005).

Catherine Hirst, Technical Consultant for this book, who also designed and created the following projects: Cold-weather scarf (p.62), Clutch bag (p.64), Lacy scarf (p.68), Bookmark (p.90), Shawl (p.92), Wrist warmers (p.94), Teddy bear (p.102), Project basket (p.104), Baby's booties (p.110), Toy balls (p.112), and Beanie hat (p.116). Catherine is a professional textiles and crafts instructor at colleges and independent studios across London, the UK, and abroad. Her work has been featured in top craft publications, including *Mollie Makes, Let's Knit, Inside Crochet, Handmade Living, Simply Crochet,* and *Crafts Beautiful.* Catherine is the author of *Teeny Tiny Crochet* (2012) and *Granny Square Crochet* (2012). Visit her at www.catherinehirst.com.

Erin McCarthy, who designed and created the Baby's blanket (p.128) and Patchwork blanket (p.130). Erin learned to crochet three years ago after longing to make beautiful crocheted blankets like those she had spied all over blogland. Crochet acts as a relaxing hobby that balances out a busy day job as a special needs teacher. Erin would like to thank Catherine Hirst for teaching her everything she knows about crochet!

Claire Montgomerie, who designed and created the Baby's cardigan (p.52), Chevron cushion (p.78), and Round cushion (p.118). She also created the Bead necklace (p.28) (Art Direction: Gemma Fletcher; Photography: Dave King) and Pretty headband (p.50) (Art Direction: Isabel de Cordova). Claire is a textiles designer who specializes in knitting and crochet, constructing fabrics, garments, creatures, and accessories that are fun, quirky, and modern. She has written many knitting and crochet books and also edits the UK craft magazine, *Inside Crochet.* Find out more at www.montyknits.blogspot.com.

Tracey Todhunter, for the Kiddy slippers (p.114) (Art Direction: Isabel de Cordova).

Original Crochet Step By Step credits
Photography: Ruth Jenkinson (except for the project credits listed to the left)
Art Direction: Glenda Fisher (except for the project credits listed to the left)
Technical Consultant: Catherine Hirst
Crochet Projects and Patterns:
Catherine Hirst, Claire Montgomerie, and Erin McCarthy